MORE TEA AT MISS CRANSTON'S

MORE TEA AT MISS CRANSTON'S

FURTHER RECOLLECTIONS OF GLASGOW LIFE

Collected and compiled by

ANNA BLAIR

Illustrated by
Bill Taylor

SHEPHEARD-WALWYN

ISBN 0-85683-127-1

Printed and bound in Great Britain
for Shepheard-Walwyn (Publishers) Ltd,
26 Charing Cross Road (Suite 34), London WC2H 0DH
by Cox & Wyman Ltd, Reading, Berkshire,
from typesetting by Alacrity Phototypesetters,
Banwell Castle, Weston-super-Mare.

Cover design by Alan Downs
based on an illustration by Bill Taylor

1st Impression September 1991

Contents

Acknowledgements

I should like to record my gratitude to all the rememberers for these pages who trustingly welcomed me and my inquisitive questions. I hope I have not let them down. I acknowledge my debt too to Bill Taylor whose sensitive illustrations make a fine contribution to the book. Warm thanks are due also to Mrs. Elizabeth Dewar for invaluable help, to Jean Matheson of Kilmartin for access to taped material, to Shepheard-Walwyn Ltd. for advice at every stage and finally, as always, to my good-humoured and encouraging husband.

To Margaret and John for long
friendship and, in the year of her
ninety-fifth birthday, to CONNIE,
who first called me a 'writer'.

Introduction

There are some periods which attract to them the name of a feature, a movement or person dominant during its timespan . . . the Churchill Era, the Iron Age, the Thatcher Years, the Enlightenment. On a more domestic scale when one speaks of the days of the Glasgow tearoom the name of Kate Cranston is the one that springs to mind, presiding, as it were, over the civic tea-pot and cakes. It conjures up a vision of part of the city's lifestyle from the 1880s to the mid-twentieth century . . . the Miss Cranston Years.

This book is not *about* Kate Cranston, but the writer was called to account after *Tea at Miss Cranston's* by a cheated reader who had expected to find in its pages a biography of that good lady. The title of that book, as of this, was meant simply to evoke a picture of those years in Glasgow when tearooms were in their heyday, when tramcars clanged and shipyards hooters sounded, when some children ran barefoot and others walked the west-end parks with nursemaids, when music-halls were popular and pavements checkered with peever beds. In short what the books contain are the recollections of elderly Glasgow men and women, of many aspects of their lives, at home, at school, at play, and on occasion (just one memory among a host of others) being taken as a treat for tea at Miss Cranston's.

Nevertheless, to appease that disappointed reader, let's set the scene with a word or two about that doyenne of the city's tea-shops, where she catered for grandmothers in bonnets with bows at the side, for little girls in trubenised collars, wearing Leghorn hats over rag-ringlets, and for small boys in velvet suits and crocheted collars (a confession from one who can look back nearly eighty years to such humiliation). And . . .

> When I went for tea at Miss Cranston's my mother would be wearing
> a long dress with a nipped-in waist and brush-braid round the hem to
> stop it getting all tattered. It was always long dresses. Y'know when
> I was a wee thing I could only see my mother's toes. I only knew she
> wore 'directoire' knickers because I saw them on the kitchen pulley.

Kate Cranston's lifetime spanned all those changing fashions.
She was born in 1849, the daughter of the owners of the Crow
Hotel in George Square. Little is recorded of her young life but
by the 1870s, seeing her tea-merchant brother Stuart offering tastes
of his different blends to his lady customers at his Argyle Street
premises she was inspired to go a step further and open her own
place below Arthur's Hotel at 114 Argyle Street, providing not
only the tea but dainty snacks and cakes, and a pleasant room in
which to linger over them. The enterprise prospered and expanded
when, as a wedding present in 1892, she was given the whole
building of Arthur's Hotel to develop, the Argyle Street area at
that time being the main shopping area of the city with Daly's still
an elegant store there.

At forty-three Kate had married John Cochrane, a Barrhead
man of thirty-five with the wealth to allow them to move in
musical and artistic circles where they met Alexander Reid, who
had lodged for a time with Van Gogh and been painted by him, the
artist brothers Walton and the young architect-designer Charles
Rennie Macintosh. Kate was also now in a position to indulge her
ideas for the fine furbishing of her home and her tearooms.

The couple settled first at 'Eastpark' in Carlibar Road, Barrhead,
a roomy semi-detached house which Kate invited George Walton's
company to decorate. After a century, the hand of his associate,
Macintosh, is still to be seen in the elegant and gracious drawing-
room, which generations of occupiers have appreciated sufficiently
to keep almost exactly as it was originally, with slender white
columns, trellis-work and stained-glass featured in the oriel
window area, with seating still upholstered in Art Nouveau fabric,
with a fine fireplace and overmantel and handsome plaster-work
on ceiling and frieze.

Kate was into her stride now. She opened a chain of tearooms and, having found the style of Rennie Macintosh in total sympathy with her own discerning taste, commissioned him to design the interiors of other strategically placed establishments like The Willow in Sauchiehall Street and those in Ingram Street, Buchanan Street and Renfield Street. Glasgow was in its great tearoom period and Cranston's egalitarian doors were open alike to suburban ladies, working-class sweethearts and maids on half-days off, all enjoying favourite rooms in the different restaurants, the White, the Green, the Dutch etc.

By now Kate and John Cochrane had taken the more imposing mansion of 'Househill' on the bank of the Levern, where they employed a large indoor and outdoor staff and also, once again, the talents of their protégé Rennie Macintosh. 'Hoozel', as the local people called the place, became a prime example of the designer's unique spacial, slender-lined and light-filled style.

There are still those in Barrhead who carry pictures of Kate, living and entertaining as the 'lady of the Big House', and setting-off for Glasgow of a morning with her husband in carriage and pair. Somewhere on the journey, it's said she shed the persona of Mrs. Cochrane and became Kate Cranston.

> Quite a wee madam she was s'posed to be at the tearooms . . . strict but fair they said she was . . . went round all her places every day and made all her staff hold out their hands for her to inspect. People said she had her kitchens white-washed every week.

It wasn't always easy to ensure total hygiene even with the nail inspection and the white-wash brush. Miss Jenny Logan once came on a Cranston rebuke to a habit which had obviously affronted Kate in the early days.

> I remember a notice in the Ladies' Room.
> 'Would ladies please refrain from combing out their hair, as there have been complaints of hair being carried away on people's skirts.'
> That must have been quite an operation to take down long hair, comb it out and put it back up again.

Tea at Miss Cranston's in Macintosh surroundings was the great

treat for upwards of half a century in the city. John Cochrane, whose circumstances had allowed this social flowering and artistic patronage to take off, died in 1917. Kate herself lived to be eighty-five and died in 1934, the very year that fire swept through and destroyed the Macintosh masterpiece at 'Househill'. Her grave is in Neilston Cemetery.

Present generations can be grateful not only that they can eat in the restored version of The Willow tearoom, but to Kate Cranston for encouraging the genius of Rennie Macintosh, letting it emerge as part of the distinctive Glasgow Style, which looks like being an enduring part of European artistic history.

Having done justice (if perhaps a little scant) to Miss Cranston, we can turn our attention in succeeding pages to the many and varied facets of the vibrant life that throbbed elsewhere in the city during her reign as Queen of the Tearooms.

1
Mixed Infants

It's a startling, if self-evident, truth when it first dawns that one is not just the next-one down in a vertical line of forebears, but the product of thirty-two great-great grandparents and sixty-four thrice-greats . . . and consequently a queer mixture of genes, personality and talent. Your 'ordinary' Glasgow man or woman is like that . . . with a dash of teuchter and teuton, latin and slav, hebrew and hibernian, anglo and asian, to spice the basic lowlander stock rooted here since the Clyde was shallow and the Tobacco Lords a scarlet novelty.

So the rememberers for this book gather-in many strands to weave the picture of Glasgow life since the turn of the century, not only from all airts of the city, but from north, south, east and west, of the world beyond.

In this opening chapter there's a kind of thumbnail index of the cheerful band who offer here their tales of life as children of Glasgow, nearly always struggling with a budget and the grime of an industrial city . . . a life sometimes hard, sometimes joyful, but always realistic. Let's name them and root them, so that in later recollections we can meet them as acquaintances already made. For those who prefer to remain anonymous a 'nom de réminiscence' has been used so that we can enjoy the memories of the bashful without making them wish they had kept themselves to themselves.

Perhaps no one has better right to first mention than Mrs. Peggy Carson, now of Ibrox.

> You couldn't get more Glasgow than my grandpa because he was born on a Fair Monday, in 1836, up the High Street. That was before Victoria was Queen, mind. My grandma was Argyle Street. Mysel' I was born and reared in Govan, at school and lived all my life there.

1

Since then she has spent all the years of her marriage and widowhood in a solid Ibrox tenement. So if birth beside the Tolbooth bell, and life in earshot of a shipyard hooter, equates to Bow Bells in London as a measure of the true native, then Peggy Carson is surely a child of St. Mungo.

Gallowgate must also lay claim to being at the core of Glasgow, and Mrs. Agnes Grove had her early days close by.

> I stayed, first, up off the Gallowgate as a child . . . in Cubie Street on the way to Camlachie, near Macfarlane's bakery. My father was a tailor and cutter and worked from the house. After Gallowgate we flitted up to Duke Street, near the school, and the church at Sidney Place and the Tennant's Brewery. My father used to say our district was Salvation, Education and Damnation, because of the church, the school and the brewery.
>
> My grandparents lived up there too and I had a great-grandmother who worked as a caretaker at some mission, Portland Street way. My husband and his father were both tenters in the silk weaving.

Further east, Miss Jenny Logan was born at the tail of last century in bien Dennistoun where her early memories are of the 'Parade' school . . . and the tragedy of her doll's pram, on the day they left that area.

> It was one of the ones with two handles instead of a bar across, two big wheels at the front and two small ones at the back. The small ones were bashed out of place at the flitting and I was heartbroken, Moving to the southside was a big change for the family but it's the broken pram that I remember. My father was a school teacher so Giffnock was just as convenient.

Another who recalls Alexandra Parade school is Mr. Struan Yule, but we have to take the tram or the three-horse 'bus (stabled in Spittal's yard) to find his birthplace at Tollcross.

> Yes, I was born there, but it was quite a long way into Dobbies Loan where my father had a cabinet-making and joinery business. (My grandfather had been a cabinet-maker too.) So when I was still quite young we moved into a tenement flat in Mackinfaulds Mansions, Dennistoun . . . a lot of rooms off a big hall with a high, fancy ceiling and a huge cupboard. I remember it was cold except in the kitchen with the big black range. It was there I went to school.

So he was brought up in Dennistoun from the time he was a Mixed Infant at the Parade school, and it was there that he watched his father build his castle in the air.

My father always had this dream of building his own home. Every week-end he used to take out his drawing-board, his double-edged and chisel-pointed pencils and work on designing this ideal house he was to put up. He never did. He eventually bought one in Burnside. But he always had that dream.

Dennistoun claims many a well-doing son and daughter, but none sturdier-spirited than Miss Janet Kay.

Dennistoun, yes. That was my part of the world, though for a time we lived near Rutherglen. I was an only child, born well before the First War and I was considered a bit delicate so I was wrapped in cotton wool. But here's me now, still going strong. My mother's family further back were handloom weavers south-west of Glasgow but the more immediate family were mill-workers come right into the city when the weaving died out. My father worked in Singer's at Clydebank.

To the south-west of the dreaming cabinet-maker and the coddled Janet was born Mr. Jack Roche in Bridgeton.

I think I would've been born in Muslin Street. But we kept flitting . . . two houses in Greenhead Street, others in James Street and Main Street. If my Pa was bringin' in a good wage my mother took a two-room- and-kitchen, if things were rough it would be a room-and-kitchen or maybe just a single-end wi' a landin' cludgie . . . and a wee black iron jawbox. It was always my Ma arranged the flits. One place I mind of, you looked out on to the Umbrella at the Cross, and from another it was the Wills's tobacco place. My father was in different jobs loading vans for warehouses. I was the only boy and my Ma was determined that when I grew up I would get a good job and go dressed to my work. That was the big thing folk boasted about, 'goin' dressed to your work'. Meant a suit an' a collar'n'tie. Status.

Born to a clay-pipe-making father, Alex Donnelly was a child of the same area though he prefers 'Calton' to Bridgeton.

They're near, but no' the same. No, no. Kent Street I was born, in 1901 near Wills's and Mitchell's tobacco places. Then I stayed in King Street close by Annie Lavery's fish shop. Everyb'dy knew Annie Lavery.

Over to the north-east of the Cathedral the ghost of a small, pinafored girl dances over Garngad Hill. Now she is Mrs. Mysie Kyle but early in the century she was the youngest of the Morton family and, unlike all the other Glasgow-born rememberers, lived in a villa rather than a tenement.

I was born in Garngad. My father had an aerated water factory there . . . lemonade and so on. It was a big cottage with cam-ceiled rooms. I was the baby of the five of us . . . two brothers and three sisters. One of my grandfathers was the lock-keeper at the canal so my father was brought up beside that. My other grandfather worked at Dalmeny House with the Earl of Rosebery . . . the race-horse people y'know. So my mother was brought up there on the estate. That would all be away back into the last century. My mother's family moved into Glasgow when she was young.

The west-end, where Miss Alison Dow lived, was a different, more rarefied kind of Glasgow than we've seen so far.

We lived off Great Western Road. My father was a lawyer in the city and we lived in a big maindoor flat. It's quite sad really but I remember my nursemaid almost better than my mother, at least when I was small. Later I was with her more, but we were never very close. Nana slept with us and gave us our meals, took us to school and out walking . . . and if you fell or got into trouble it was always Nana you went to. Except Sundays. Then my mother and father took us to my grandmother's after church. Sometimes in the afternoon she sent for a carriage and we went for what she called 'an airing. I suppose I don't know much about real Glasgow life . . .

Then the ninety-year-old head cocks to the side . . .

. . . unless, of course, my kind of life was just a different slice of Glasgow.

Perhaps she's right, for another whose memories are of the west-end and its wide crescents and avenues, its social cachet and gracious social round, is Mrs. Millicent Davis . . . yet her background family-profession was Glasgow, root and branch.

Both my parents were Glasgow, born in the 1870s . . . and my paternal grandparents before that. There's been a long family connection with Fairfield's Yard. My husband was with the company, my father was chief engine designer and my grandfather was works manager. Our life was all to the west of the city. I was born in Marlborough Avenue, then we went to Old Kilpatrick for a while and later came back into the west-end.

Mr. James Dewar was born in King's Park . . .

. . . at my granny's house because my father was away. He was a trader along the West African coast in the early years of the century . . . very little at home. Then for about four years I went to Rothesay. So I was a wee Ro'say boy at first, watching the electric trams and putting down farthings on the rails to make ha'pennies. But I really began to be Glasgow when we came back to a tenement in Cartvale Road. Mother was a midwife there. She always wanted a garden so eventually we moved to Auldburn Road in Pollokshaws. It was 'country' then, and she loved the country. I remember the rasp of the corncrakes there, the open fields and roaming away up the burn.

Long before young Jimmy was wandering there, Ann Hutchison was born in the older, central part of Pollokshaws, and passes a sad little judgement on her arrival.

I was born at 45, Pleasance Street near the shirt factory and the kippering store. I was the baby . . . the one that wasnae wanted. Th'was two that died in infancy and other ten, George, Sam, Davy and Thomas . . . and five girls, Mary, Lizzie, Meg, then Jeanie-that-brought-me-up, and myself. We'd what you call a main-door, not a close . . . th'was only two of these in the street. We'd a front door with a back door and a back close. And we'd *lovely* windows, curtains an' that. It was a room and kitchen, with a coal fire in the room and the range in the kitchen. My Daddy kept the range lovely. That was his job in the house. His right work though, was going round with his horse and cart selling logs, fire sticks and coal briquettes.

In the first decade of the century there began to be migration to the suburbs of people who could manage to buy rather than rent, and Miss Isobel Horn's family was part of that.

I was born in a tenement in Shawlands, but my brother was ill at one point and the doctor advised living somewhere higher. So we went to Giffnock three miles away. My grandmother lived in the same road.

The First War was then blighting the prospects of marriage for the young women of that generation . . .

My mother was one of ten, and the only girl to get married. There were four young unmarried aunts over in my grandmother's and she was very much the head of that house. My family was in whisky broking.

From the same district come recollectios of another war . . . of Mr. Hamish Thomson's R.A.F. days as a 'teenager and years as a prisoner-of-war. And his wife Mrs. Helen Thomson speaks of the watershed in her suburban life brought to it by active service in the A.T.S.

Perhaps the most intriguing nest for Glasgow-born-and-bred fledgings to fly, was that in McLean Street, Govan, where the Rodgers sisters, Christina and Mary, were born in the first decade of the century. Chrissie, now Mrs. Ronnie, speaks first.

We were a big family . . . twelve of us (with the two that died young)
. . . five boys and five girls left. It was a two-room-and-kitchen tenement
house and my mother had a farm through the back.

Then Mary, now Mrs. Brisbane . . .

There was a close through to the back court, th'was stables there and a
dung midden and our three/four cows. And we'd chickens. My mother
had come from Greenock and I think she'd worked on a farm there. The
farm at the back and the dairy she ran on the front street was her work.
My father driv the big Finnieston cran.

There's a fading photograph on a table, of a young woman in that
back-court, fine-featured, with lively intelligent eyes, carrying a
milking stool and a wooden bucket, standing beside a cow with
curling horns. She wears a plain round-necked shirt, sleeves
rolled up, with a long coarse skirt and apron . . . and she is
quite beautiful.

That's Mother going to milk the cows.

And that's your sure-as-death, Clyde-built Glasgow bodies . . .
some pure-bred, some with a gene or two from a far forebear come
long ago to the town. But over this present century the city has
absorbed varying tides of incomers who have greatly enriched the
community, bringing style and talent, exotic tastes and customs,
drive, energy and culture to colour life in every corner of the city.
Some made quite short journeys to settle here . . . Mr. Robert Ford
from no further than Portpatrick.

I was born in Portpatrick in 1905. My father worked on a farm
there and had his own wee croft as well. I left school at twelve.
(You could do that in the First War when they were hard-up
for farm workers). It was hard-hard work, five in the morning
to seven or eight at night. Too hard. So I learned my trade
as a joiner and later came to Glasgow. I've been here ever
since.

Portpatrick is the place where the saint once left his footprint
after crossing the Irish Sea in a single stride. Less miraculously,
Mrs. Eileen Reilly's parents made their journey by boat, to be
Glasgow immigrants around the time of the First War.

Both my parents came over from Ireland. Separately. My father came from Armagh, to improve his prospects and because of what seemed, even then, like never-ending Irish troubles. He became a passenger-guard on the railway here. His sister came too, with a friend. The friend became my mother because when there was some talk of her going on to North America my father got a move on and proposed.

The two immigrants began the task of house-hunting.

In those days you needed 'key money' (that was just a back-hander to the factor). So until they'd saved that up they went into digs . . . the attic of a big house in West Street, and that's where I was born. My mother took me back to see it later. Not much of a place, but I think if you've come from a background where your parents have had it hard and made sacrifices for you, you should be proud to talk about that.

Mrs. Bunty Angles had a sadder start to life.

I was born in the Isle of Man then my parents went off to a job in Africa and left me with my granny in Glasgow. They were to collect me on their first trip home when I was a wee bit bigger. But my mother died out there and I just stayed on with my granny . . . never knew my mother. My granny stayed in a room-and-kitchen in Mount Street.

Then things looked up . . . by one vital apartment.

We moved to a room-and-kitchen with *an inside toilet*.

. . . and progressed to having a proper bedroom.

Yes, the next move was to a two-room-and-kitchen and we lived with my aunt and her new husband. My granny used to go out as a midwife.

Such were the transplants from adjacent towns and islands, some of them no doubt traumatic enough. But other incomers had more daunting decisions to make before they threw in their lot with the 'dear green place', with its different climate and language and utterly strange lifestyles. Pogroms and poverty were powerful springboards for Mrs. Lily Joseph's family, although at first it was a build-up of unhappy circumstances that propelled her mother at least, into a foreign future.

My mother's father in Russia was very very comf'table . . . a big house and their own horse and trap. He went round farms buying up oats. But his wife died at my mother's birth and it was a housekeeper brought her up. My mother liked the housekeeper and she loved her father, but then he married again and she never settled with her stepmother. So she married the first man that came along just to get away . . . married beneath her, that's what they said. I don't know. Anyway they'd two baby boys there, and then because of the pogrom in 1897 they set out for America. They'd to come third class, below decks, but that didn't hinder them. When they arrived at Liverpool they thought it was America. But they just stayed, and later came to Glasgow and my father got work in the cigarette factory close to where they lived in the Gorbals. That was in Adelphi Street. I was the eighth to be born there . . . right at the tail end. By that time they were well into being Glasgow from head to toe.

Head to toe maybe, but not to tongue.

Mind you, my parents always conversed in Yiddish and while they were alive we were bi-lingual, but then it dropped off. All their folks were still in Russia but they lost touch in the next generation. I'm just Glasgow. All my life Glasgow's been good to me.

East European rumblings were in the background of another who knew Yiddish as her home tongue, Mrs. Lily Balarsky.

My mother and father were both immigrants from Vilna in Lithuania. It was a college town . . . 'Vilnius' they call it on the B.B.C. When my father was a boy at the end of last century, young men were being forced into the army and Jews in the army had a bad time . . . anti-semitism y'know. So quite a lot decided to come west. America was the Mecca. But my parents just got on a boat, came first into Scotland and stayed here . . . settled in Glasgow. 'Getting on a boat' was a sort of jargon for going away as emigrants or refugees . . . they really didn't know where. It was a big adventure I suppose. They spoke Yiddish so there was the language thing to cope with too. It's not much used now, Yiddish, but I belong to a group called the Friends of Yiddish and on a Sunday afternoon we have readings from the Jewish classics, Sholem Aleichem or Sholem Asch. It's nostalgic and it's very expressive . . . some German, Slav, Romany and Hebrew in it. It was common to Latvia, Estonia and Lithuania so it kind of bound the immigrants together in those old days.

Lily's father bought small goods and a suitcase, set himself up as a travelling salesman and did the rounds of country villages with his wares.

> My mother came from Vilna too. Things in Lithuania had been bad for every one, especially Jews. My grandmother was a widow and could hardly support her family. So my mother and her sister 'got on a boat' too, and landed in Glasgow. They got lodgings in a part of the Saltmarket where a lot of Jewish people lived when they first came . . . d'you know Skipka Pass?

Both girls met their husbands in the city.

> There were social meeting-places for the immigrants. My mother and father met there.

On his peddling travels the Jewish salesman had taken a notion to the country town of Cumnock and after they married the young couple stayed there with the suitcase for a year or two until Lily was born. But life was strange without a Jewish community . . .

> . . . so we came back and settled up a close in Stockwell Street

Unrest and poverty further south in Europe, in Italy, perhaps as a legacy from the Garibaldi period, brought another enriching influx to towns all over Britain, with waves of Italians coming to seek their fortunes, or at least a modest competence, here. Glasgow may have been a little suspicious at first, but has never had cause to regret their arrival. It's a poor row of shops that doesn't have its café or chippie, and a fair bet that if it has, it's run by Glasgow Italians of the second or third generation of a dynasty . . . like Mr. Angelo Lamarra.

> One side of the family was originally from Tuscany. My mother's people. It's a lovely part in the north.

And this most genial of Glasgow-Italians has a photograph of his mother's home village among the folding mountains of North Italy, beside the cash-desk of his Glasgow restaurant.

> Beautiful . . . but there wasn't much work there so they moved south at the turn of the century to farm work there. My father lived in the south at that time, near Monte Cassino. My parents met there and got

married. They were of big families . . . too big to give a living to all the sons, so my mother and father came to Scotland and all the family was born here. They settled first at Stenhousemuir (and y'know it's a funny thing . . . all my life, though I've never seen them play, I've always supported Stenh'smuir football club . . . the first result I look for every Saturday). Anyway we'd a fish-and-chip shop there, so I've been in the same trade all my days.

But now Angelo presides over the spacious and popular city-centre Trees Restaurant in Union Street.

My father died when I was still young and things came to be very hard so my mother brought us to Steven Street at St. George's Cross. That was us into Glasgow and I've been happy here ever since. There was the war and internment of course. That was a wee bit difficult. But it passed.

Other arts and skills arrived with the Italian community. Mr. Mario Servadei's background story is similar to that of Angelo Lamarro's . . . even to the Tuscany mother. But his craft is different.

My father came from near Rimini on the Adriatic side. The farm holdings were small . . . not big enough for a lot of sons. So one young fellow would come here, get started and then send for another . . . and another. My father had been a shoemaker over there, then learned the hairdressing in Genoa. My grandfather made barrels for the wine trade, so there were a few skills in the family. My mother's brothers came and opened a small café on the south side, and when they went into the army in the First War she came from Italy to keep the café going. So that was her here. My father'd come to work for an uncle who was a hairdresser in Clydebank. Later he opened a place of his own. He met my mother with some Italian friends. They married, settled in Glasgow and I was born in a tenement in Daisy Street So I was real Italian-Glasgow from birth.

That then is the cast of this book. There are others who have thrown in their tuppence-worth to a chapter here and there, just eaves-dropping in an eventide home lounge, dropping remarks at parties, or in casual 'bus encounters; but since their appearances are as 'extras' only and not as stars, we can simply meet them as they cross our paths.

2

I Couldn't Sing for Toffee

A gazateer of 1881 gives a certain Edinburgh school a pat on the back for innovation recording that 'the changing from room to room is effected to music five minutes before each hour . . . showing a model of organisation'. It's a second-hand memory of that same institution, founded in 1695, that is the earliest in this chapter.

> My granny stayed with her grandparents in Edinburgh and went to the Merchant Maidens' school there. That was because her father had been a cooper in Leith, but he'd died when she was young, so she was considered to be an orphan and the school was for the daughters of deceased tradesmen.

That sad little tale of the 'other' city may not seem to hold much place among Glasgow memories but it does deserve the passing observation that that guardian great-great-grandmother of Miss Isobel Horn's must have had her own education, however much or little, in the time of George III or at least in that of one of Queen Victoria's wicked uncles, George IV or William IV.

But let's leave the Edinburgh Maidens and sift through the school memories of Isobel's own Glasgow contemporaries.

It may not be the three Rs that are recalled with the greatest affection when the elderly talk of their classroom days, but since these Rs were dinned into them as thoroughly as the Shorter Catechism perhaps we should begin with them. Little Eileen Duffy's school at Tollcross might have been purpose planned to daunt a timid 'only'.

I'd no brothers or sister to tell me what school would be like . . . to *warn* me. I went to St. Marks at first. It was traditional . . . very old-fashioned methods . . . chanting the alphabet and saying 'Cee-Ai-Tee spells cat' instead of sounding it out. And the teacher pointed out letters on the board. We did everything to numbers. On 1! you stood up. On 2! you moved into the passage. On 3! you lowered your hinged seat. On 4! you stood up on the seat. Then you chanted the letters to her pointer and you got it across the legs if you were wrong.

Eileen was not going to knuckle under to that without showing a little spirit.

I tried to run away and the teacher put a boy each side of me to make me stay put. Then I tried putting my hand up to get out, the way I saw others doing for the toilet . . . and that was another chase.

But there was a more enlightened regime at her next school where the Montessori System of teaching had arrived.

As far as the reading was concerned, I soon got the hang of sounding out the words (although at five I thought the new teacher just didn't know any better). But I stayed a kind of poor speller for a while with the mixture of the Cee-Ai-Tee and the phonetics.

And the later English graduate produces a childhood scribble in one of her old books C.R.O.C.A.D.L.E., written beside a tale of adventure on the Nile.

One who could have done with the improvement Eileen Duffy later showed, was the labourer remembered by surveyor Tom Marchant.

This chap was sent out to a building site to check amounts of materials stored. He scribbled the amount on a scrap of paper . . . 100 wat son. And came back. 'What's this?' says I. 'A hunnerweight san'' (1 cwt sand) says-he, as if it was me that was daft. Another time we got 'joist' spelt J.O.Y.C.E.

Mario Servadei was never as bad as that, but confesses that *he* wasn't great at the spelling either.

Italian was what I heard at home and you just spell it the way it sounds. Well, you can't very well do that with English. But y'see *I* tried. And got a bit confused. I got kept back for my spelling. So was another boy and he wasn't Italian. Funny enough though, he became a reporter on

The Glasgow Herald and I used to ask him, 'Who does your spelling for you now, Charlie?'

One of an assortment of rememberers who attended the 'Parade' School between the late 1890s and the First War was little Jenny Logan.

When I first went to school in Alexandra Parade, I was in a great big room with the Infant Mistress Miss Towers in the middle, and a pupil teacher at each end. (They were maybe from the Normal School. That was the teacher-training college at that time).

In Struan Yule's time at Alexandra Parade school, Miss Hunter was the first teacher.

She was a terror, but she could teach. And there was a Miss Walker who played the piano for us all to march like troops in the door and up the stairs. I remember her playing 'Blaze Away'. The piano was down in the corner of the stair-well, really what passed for a hall.

'Blaze Away' was recalled by another Parade infant.

Oh yes, fine. But there was a Sousa march as well and the big boys used to march in singing their own words to that . . . under their breath mind.
'All of a sudden a big mealie pudden'
Came flying through the air' . . .

I never knew the rest of it, if there *was* any more. Struan Yule remembers learning to write and, in common with every other who ever wielded slate and slate-pencil, still grues at the scree-eeech of pencil on surface, and remembers the special stone sill in the playground where they sharpened the points of their 'pinsels'.

They had a quieter way of learning their letters in Jimmy Dewar's school at Battlefield.

We'd Miss Burns at first, followed by Miss Carlyle, a small diminutive figure in black button boots. When we were very wee we formed our letters in trays of sand . . . made a mess with the sand mind you, but it must've been quite economical. You just rubbed it smooth again after the teacher came round and saw you'd done it right.

Counting methods were neither so ingenious nor so progressive.

> First you sat with your back bolt-upright, then you recited the tables
> . . . up to twelve times. If anyone doubts that was an ideal way to learn
> to multiply they've just to ask you thirteen times this or that, and you
> cannae do it. I'm always foozled after the twelve times. It was maybe
> old-fashioned, but it worked.

They didn't use the sand for written sums though.

> We'd slates for that, and the usual wee smelly rag in a tin, that you spat
> on to wipe the slate.

Mysie Kyle at Rosemount School had her sums from Miss
Clenaghan . . .

> . . . you'd to do your sums on boards all round the walls and the
> teacher stood behind you with the belt.

Another octogenarian still smarts at the thought of that belt.

> Nothin'to dae wi' you were good or bad behaved. Just you maybe
> couldnae dae your seven-times. Diabolical liberty it was to get hit for
> that!

Pointers seem to have been as much weapons as teaching
implements. Bunty Angles remembers fidgets and chattering
that merited a wee rap from one of her first teachers. She recalls
the grim rule of the janitor too, although *he* wasn't armed except
by a large pair of hands.

> It was the jannie ruled the playground and chased you into your lines.
> He could just about lift some of the big boys with one hand.

As well as sand-trays and screaming slates, there were pot-
hooks and jotters, with urgings to take your pencil 'up light
and down heavy', and then all the blotty intricacies of joined-up
writing in ink with a nib. But there was one teaching aid that
did a double turn by offering a grounding in proverb as well as
copperplate. Vere Foster copy-books, of the Art Nouveau-covers
and age-old wisdom, are recalled with respect, if not affection.

> Vere Foster . . . some of us quite liked our Vere Fosters but some
> couldnae be bothered. 'A Rolling Stone Gathers No Moss' or

'Discretion is the Better Part of Valour'. You'd maybe get that on the top line of a page and you'd to copy it better and better on the lines below that.

Not all remembered schools were your School Board Elementaries.

My school was a wee bit different. It was a room in the Langside Halls at the Queen's Park in Shawlands. I'm going back now to about 1907. I'd be about five when I started. Well, there was just the one class and Miss Sharpe took it . . . all ages up to big school age, about ten. We'd little desks and she taught us in groups . . . one lot getting on with work by themselves while she gave a lesson to another. None of this playing yourself with bricks, and calling it 'learning'. None of that nonsense. It was a private school, about twenty children but, for all it was wee, we were well up in everything. The older ones even had the beginnings of French. She was strict was Miss Sharpe, but she was nice . . . Once she cuddled me into her when I fell, and when I held my breath she thought I was in shock. But–here it was only because of the moth-balls in her clothes. I remember my two years at that wee school better than the eight I had at big school.

Isobel Horn was at another Dame School.

At first I was at the local school, but just for two weeks, because I got the belt from the Infant Mistress for swooping about like an aeroplane. So I got my wee palmy. My parents weren't very pleased, so they sent me instead to Miss Gardner's wee private school at Ingleneuk. It was just a cottage really with a kind of big shed at the back where the school was. We all sat at a big round table . . . all ages, and Miss Gardner taught us. She wore a long grey skirt and a high-necked blouse with stiff cuffs.

Miss Gardner had no strap. She had worthier, more personal sanctions at her disposal . . . She had Presence. She was neither cosy nor lovable but she could teach and she could quell a miscreant with a word or glance, and total order reigned at Ingleneuk.

We sat at this table doing set work, and were kind of divided into stages . . . maybe three or four in each. When your 'class' was called you trooped over to stand round Miss Gardner in her chair in a corner. We all learned quite well there, but I never mastered 'notation'. Do you remember notation . . . putting the commas in for tens and hundreds and thousands? She was strong on manners too, Miss Gardner.

Perhaps the most unlikely location for schooling was a church tower used before there was a local public school building in the area.

> There were two small rooms with fires. If you were good you got to put on the coals. There was a toilet and wash-hand basin outside the door of each room. I left there eighty-six years ago but I remember it fine, quite different from the big Dennistoun school I'd been at before that.

For a few more years pinafores, button-boots and Norfolk jackets went up that spiral stair for lessons and played in the kirk yard, before the whole complement of two teachers and perhaps two dozen children was moved to a temporary but purpose-built, corrugated school quarter of a mile away.

> That was the Tin Academy. I got a prize at the Tin Academy . . . for tidiness. That was well over eighty years ago.

Miss Mabel Logan has lived with little Jenny's tidiness for a long time.

> She's still tidy. The only tidy one in the family.

Neat, she may have been . . .

> But I wasn't very academic . . . diligent maybe . . . but not academic.

That's a self-calumny for she was academic enough later to take a double Maths degree as one of Glasgow University's very early women students.

As well as the rote learning (some of it enjoyed in a way perhaps incomprehensible now when the education process has to be not only relevant and self-expressive but 'fun' as well) there were also domestic skills, social and artistic graces imparted long ago. Mrs. Lily Joseph was introduced to the first at her Gorbals schools.

In our family it was Buchan Street and Adelphi Street school we went to. I learned to darn at school, along with everything else.

Her teacher killed two birds with one stone when she discovered young Lily's skill with bodkin.

I was the darner in our class and the teacher brought in all her darning for me to do. I was daft enough to be honoured. We learned to knit too.

But properly honoured she must have been half-a-century or more later, by her family.

D'you know I've knitted *eight* shawls in two-ply Shetland for the babies in our family.

To the cognoscenti the knitting of *one* two-ply shawl is an achievement of high plain-and-purling order. *Eight* is cottage industry.

Mrs. Agnes Grove learned to knit too . . . at Tureen Street school.

The first thing you knitted were your own garters . . . twelve stitches wide . . . you knitted that up and measured it round your leg until it was long enough.

Perhaps an early step in learning to sew were the cards handed out at the little Ingleneuk dame school.

These cards had had holes punched in them and you'd to lace threads in and out. The stitches made texts and I think they got sent to a mission.

Pious little workers loved the cards, the rest tholed them as they tholed the redoubtable lady who ran the school.

For the boys, an advance on pulling wool through cards were the raffia shopping-bags the boys in Mario Servadei's class made and took home to their mothers. For the girls, as soon as small female fingers were supple enough, there came the dreaded 'specimens', the shoe-bags edged with cross-stitch and the lap-bags that portended gloomy years of school 'seams' ahead. But the shoe-bag, at least, was a symbol of the better-loved 'drill'.

You were in lines according to your height for drill. We'd the smallest boy I'd ever seen in my life in our class, Harold Brett. He was always at the front . . . two rows of boys, two of girls . . . then all the orders . . . Hips . . . firm! Arms . . . bend! Head . . . up!

Sometimes it was just the jannie who presided over the drill, reckoned to be well up in that sort of thing after his years in the army. Even if there was no hall, or much other space, for the jannie to hark back to his military days, all was not lost.

In our single room school at Langside Halls, at some stage every day the teacher would stop us all from our work and get us to stand up and do drill just at our seats. We'd head and arm exercises, moving and bending and turning our trunks left and right. Just cleared our heads and suppled us up.

Those were the physical jerks of school life but there was also the gentler art of dancing where that was possible . . . even at Ingleneuk cottage . . .

. . . what Miss Gardner taught us was probably just singing games with hopping-about bits.

But it was a preparation for greater things, and certainly by the 1930s older boys and girls were galumphing about getting ready for school Christmas parties . . . Military two-stepping, Dashing the White Sergeant and Waltzing the Valeta.

I was a bit stooky, more of a clod-hopper . . . didnae *sway* enough. But I clumped my way through and, mind you, it's been useful ever since. D'you mind all the twirlin' in the Pride of Erin and hooching when you were at the far end fae the teacher. She could never find who hooched.

There came a less innocent day when the early disco-dancing young thought nothing of a quiet canoodle behind the sheds. And yet one teacher of those days recalls the protest when she lined up a class for their first dancing-lesson.

Aw naw, Miss. No' that! yon haudin'-on-to-each-other kinda dancin'. Naw, naw!

In spite of such rebellion many a wedding, even yet, is the livelier for the learning of hauding-on-to-each-other dancing in reluctant youth.

The other arts had their place too even in the early days of compulsory schooling. Apples, books and drapes were set up as 'still life' and tongues licked lips in the effort to get them right.

Oh aye. You fair agonised to get the two sides of some ugly vase the same. And if you done them right they got pinned up on the wall . . . and there was yon wee kinda stick figures you did, like . . . what was his name . . . Lowry? That was because you couldnae help it . . . no' like him that *meant* it!.

Perhaps for most rememberers it is the school musical efforts that stick in the mind.

We'd little songs at Langside eighty-odd years ago.
    How many miles to fairyland?
    Anyone call tell,
    Up one flight, to the right,
    Please to ring the bell.
. . . a nonsense rhyme, but I thought it was lovely and I sang it lustly.

And Mrs. Agnes Grove found her gift for singing a happy and profitable little talent at Cubie Street school.

D'you mind how you used to sing in the class at Christmastime, in wee concerts? You got a sweetie for doing it. Well, my grandma was a great one for teaching me songs and I once sang one of hers. Part of it went like this . . .
    She wouldnae leave her Mammy
    And she wouldnae leave her Daddy
    But noo she's left the both of them
    For a hurdy-gurdy laddie.
That's all I can mind now but I must've been good because I got taken to the class next door to sing it there. So that was *two* sweeties!

One who was less accomplished but just as enthusiastic, was young Eileen Duffy.

I couldn't sing for toffee, but all the kind of well-doing children (of whom I may say I was one) got into the school choir. So I just went along and mouthed the words without singing: One day when the teacher came round to listen she came to me. 'Eileen Duffy, you're opening your mouth but there's not a word coming out.' So I was sent back to my own teacher as red's a beetroot, and-here the next practice I wasn't going to go, but the teacher just sent me along to enjoy myself and I went and did my goldfish thing, opening and shutting my mouth at the right time.

For those who could't sing for toffee, or were only clod-hopping dancers, there was always 'poentry' . . . mostly taken after Silent Reading on a Friday afternoon. There can't be many who went through school without thrilling to the courage of Barbara Frietchie in the American Civil War.

> Up from the meadows rich with corn
> Into the cool September morn
> The clustered spires of Frederick stand
> Green-walled by the hills of Maryland

. . . or who doesn't recall the tearing and shooting down of the Union flags and poles, and the old woman leaning out of her window waving the last one herself and challenging the enemy leader, General 'Stonewall' Jackson?

> 'Shoot if you must, this old grey head
> But spare your country's flag,' she said.
> A shade of sadness, a blush of shame
> Over the face of the leader came . . .
> 'Who touches a hair of yon grey head
> Dies like a dog. March on!' He said.

And many a one who met Barbara Frietchie eighty years ago, can still rattle off whole verses of her story. Fine visual stuff!

A haunting poem of schooldays that appealed to Mrs. Eileen Reilly in her Duffy days, perhaps more than to others who didn't have her fey Irish background was an old cradle song. It called for quietness for a sleeping child, and protection from the peaty fumes of a winter night.

> O men from the fields come gently within
> Tread softly, softly, men coming in . . .
> From the reek of the smoke and the cold of the floor
> And the peering of things across the half-door
> O men from the fields, softly, softly come through
> Mary puts round her mantle of blue.

You see I used to go to my great-grandmother's cottage in Ireland for the holidays and there was the cold floor and peat-reek there, *and* the half-door, and when you'd been brought up like me on ghoulie stories . . . you could just see 'the peering of things' across that half-door, and the trees with their dark outlines changing in the dusk.

It was a long day at school from nine until four, making letters, doing your gizinties and spouting poetry. But there were breathers . . . interludes of one kind or another that leavened the hours. There was *resting*. Peggy Carson did that in style.

D'you mind of putting your hands behind your head with your elbows out like wings, to rest your head. Or another way was to put your head on the desk. Once when I was wee I fell asleep like that.

Another welcome interruption to routine was for the class photograph, to be immortalised in sepia with your tie-knot under one ear, your Kirby grip or your ringlets over your eyes. There may have been neat well-groomed little pussies . . . but they were never you.

In the early days of the century there was a German photographer went round the schools. His name was Volgemuth but we called him 'Wiggly-mooth'.

'Wiggly-mooth' ducked under his black cloth in Miss Jenny Logan's day until the First War when he prudently packed his tripod and disappeared from the scene. For a long time afterwards it was Mr. Prophet's photographs that were carried home. Then sadly the day of the class photo was done, in came the studio-type individual portrait and one of the nostalgic joys of putting names to wee bun faces in future middle-age was lost.

There was another break in routine which could be had for the asking, and not even the most awesome teacher could gainsay the need.

One of the things I mind about our school was the toilets . . . just a row of dry closets under a wooden board with holes in it . . . and how you used to sit there and lean sideways and skelp the bottom coming through the next hole.

In a more sophisticated establishment the W.C.s flushed and had

doors to them, though seldom with satisfactory bolts . . . so that when there was a rush at playtime . . .

. . . your best pal 'held the door'.

'Holding the door' was as much a duty of best-friendship as sharing your play-piece or being your partner in the lines. With regard to the toilet of course shrewder operators timed their 'calls' to come during lessons and did not waste good playing time.

Little Mary Rodger had a kind of dispensation for being a minute or two late each morning for these marching-in lines. She was from the dairy-farm in McLean Street.

> I used to take the teachers' milk for their tea with me to the school. I got their key and took it into their room. I got paid for it on a Friday.

That was in the days long before there was school milk for pupils.

After that there were spare third-pints a-plenty for the staffroom and even an odd one for home, so that wags could claim to recognise your average teacher anywhere on the street . . .

. . . wi' a soor face, a bashed case and a wee bottle of milk!

No chapter on Glasgow schools can close without passing reference to the fact that Roman Catholic children are educated separately from the others. There has been the odd fracas from time to time between the two camps, but on the whole there has been give-and-take.

The children from the Catholic school in Govan opposite the Protestant church used to watch for funerals to the kirkyard then go later and take flowers from the graves to put them at their own altar . . .

Give-and-take . . . or maybe take-and-give.

We'll let Mary Rodger, the milk bearer, draw the curtain on early school years with a glimpse of her sister Effie, who seems to have had the kind of rapport not many claim to have had with the teachers of their day.

One of the teachers was very fond of Effie, and when she left the school that Miss Kay gave her *two shillings*. That was a lot of money then. She was nice, Miss Kay, and y'know our Effie kept that florin till the day she died.

3
Three in the Hurlie Bed

In the years before half the city sprawled outwards into suburbia, the near million souls who seethed all day on Glasgow streets disappeared like ants into anthills by night, and life transferred itself just as vibrantly into one, two, three or more rooms-and-kitchen and umpteen single ends. Great spawns of children vanished into the maws of tenement closes and numbers lodged there far exceeded the old legal limits.

> When I was wee it was a single-end we had. Th'was two of these to each landing and two houses with two rooms . . . th'was four landings altogether. That's twenty-four rooms if I coont up, and there must've been three dozen weans in the close . . . for a' th'was a wee brass token at the doors that marked the number th'was s'posed to have been. Nob'dy paid any heed. You'd your inshot bed and a hurlie underneath and one of yon kitchen chairs that folded down. Th'was three of us in that hurlie. No bathroom mind.

Ann Hutchison too remembers the single end.

> When my sister Jeanie got married they rented a house, just a single room. The people in these houses had toilets out on the green. No bathrooms.

Life was a little more gracious with two apartments. There was the extra press-bed of course for the overspill of sleepers, but there was also the pleasant sense that visitors could be welcomed without a blush. The kitchen was still the heart though.

> It was a grand warm room that, with the fire on all night. We kept the dross and the briquettes in there too, handy. My father and mother had the kitchen bed. Th'was a toty-wee scullery too and the zinc bath hung on the wall there.

The amazing thing about the room-and-kitchen was that you really lived in the *kitchen* . . . hardly used the Room. It was for best. Kitchens weren't poky mind. You'd have scrubbed table and chairs and an armchair at the range. But the Room was special and nob'dy thought it was funny that you didn't make use of your space just for living instead of showing off. Mind you, it taught you that hospitality was important, and taking care of your nice things. Prepared you for the day, if it ever came, when you might have a big house, a three-apartment maybe. P'raps even wi' a bathroom and toilet.

For the present there were kettles and the jaw-box for washing.

We'd swan-neck taps at the sink in our room-and-kitchen in Cubie Street. Brass they were, and you could hinge them down and put a board over the sink for a kind of working top.

Niceties like keeping the Room *good* were not possible when the family was nine or ten.

We'd two big iron beds in the Room, forbye the one in the press. The girls were in the press and the boys were in the Room. I don't mind how we all got dressed, but there was certainly no jinkin' about and hidin' fae each other.

When the family had flown the coop, or if Grandma lived next door and could take some in as 'sleepers', the bed-recess could take on a whole new life of its own . . . as Mrs. Grove's father used it.

He was a tailor. He worked in the house and stored his things in the bed-press. My sister and I slept with my Grandma next door . . . for years. *Lived* in our own place but slept at hers.

Mrs. Agnes Grove remembers the move to their two-rooms-and-kitchen.

Big-big rooms they were. Th'was the kitchen bed of course, and the kind of more private press-bed with the door in the parlour. In the bedroom (oh but my mother was proud of that bedroom!) there was a brass bedstead, but you could easy have had two beds in there. There was no bathroom. We'd just to take the tin bath and put it on the toilet floor and carry hot water to it, then tim the water down the toilet. People kept themselves very clean like that. But what a skiddle. All the same you had to. As the saying goes 'maun dae's a guid master'! That house belonged to the publican at the close-mouth . . .

Eventually, after the owner put in a hot water system there was no more fetching and carrying of water in the black kettles.

A sink with two taps . . . my, that was luxury!

For Jean Paterson, another of the two-room-and-kitchen gentry, to be able to walk into a room that existed only for sleeping was fairy-tale stuff. Not that there was much 'walking into' theirs . . . certainly not by the children.

I don't remember *ever* just walking into my parents' room with its gas fire and its bed po'nds and the marble-top wash-stand. That wash-stand was the pride of my Ma's heart, with its ewer and basin in a yellow rose pattern. I might go in to help turn the mattress and so on, but apart from that it was special and you kep' out. It was a lovely room.

Two-rooms-and-kitchen were considered good houses and represented a certain social standing, especially if the family was small.

My mother had a maid in our two-room-and-kitchen. There was just me and my sister. We had the Room bed and my parents the bedroom so the maid was quite snug in the kitchen inshot.

Even so, not all such houses had mod-cons. Ann Hutchison recalls theirs in Pleasance Street.

We'd a beautiful toilet . . . nicer than lots . . . all painted on the floor, and we'd a paraffin lamp hanging and a toilet roll on the back of the door. We done it out twice't a week, put in a new toilet-roll an' that. But we'd no bath in the house. You just had the tin tub at the fire. There was a wee bath-house in Macdougall Street with just a few baths in cubicles. It was an old neighbour of ours ran it . . . that was all he could do for he'd a wooden leg from the war. You got red soap, but their towels were rough and scratchy. Nice folk took their own towels.

Here and there, there were bathrooms. But being posh had its own dangers. Mrs. Lily Joseph recalls an incident in theirs.

Ours was a small, dark bathroom in Adelphi Street with a gas geyser. You lit that with a match or a taper. One day, though, there was a terrible to-do. My sister had been gassed. They did get her out in time but they never used that geyser again. We went to the public baths in Gorbals after that.

Another of those afterthought, cupboard-sized bathrooms in the
same area, with only a tiny grille on to the close, was also the
scene of an accident.

> It was that dark and you couldnae see. You'd just a candle in wi' you
> and if there was a draught through the grille the flame got wheeched
> out. Anyway this day my mother skited on the soap and broke her
> arm. Mind, it gave her a rest for a wee while for she was never still.

That bather too, found her way to the public baths after that, for
the weekly scrub . . . a delight found earlier by Lily Balarsky and
her mother.

> We didn't have a bathroom in Stockwell Street. My mother and I went
> to the Gorbals baths once a week . . . as much hot water as you wanted.
> Great!

If you were young and learning to swim you could have a bath, of
a kind, after your dip.

> You went into the wee row of foot-tubs and you and your pal took
> three of them. You sat in tubs facing each other wi' the extra bath in
> between, and you both put your feet in it. You sat there slipping the
> carbolic soap down under your costume and slid it about . . . squirted
> it out at the top and down your back. You got a rare bath that way for
> there was no right bath at home. My mother was kinda torn between
> bein' feart I would get fleas or lice and pleased I was gettin' a good
> soapin'.

A quite different service recalled by Mrs. Mysie Kyle answered the
washing need when there was no home bath.

> Lever Brothers had portable baths. They used to put them up in school
> playgrounds. I saw them down Kelvinhaugh way. A big canvas kind
> of tent erection. The children came out of school, went in there for
> their bath and came out at the other end. That went on for quite a long
> time.

That was the accommodation in the tenement house and the use
made of it, with the excursion to the baths for those past the size
for a tubbing in the tin bath.

There was sturdy furniture and essential utensils on the household scene too, with chiffonières, what-nots, lobby coat-stands and

the wide chest of drawers for laying out suits and dresses, where the family didn't rise to a wardrobe. These along with built-in beds and dressers, with washing-boards, carpet-beaters, toasting forks, bolt-irons, tattie-champers and spirtles, were standard equipment, however many rooms forbye the kitchen. Only in bric-a-brac did imagination and personal taste have free rein. There were tea caddies, presents from everywhere, fairings, dresser-plates, crotcheted anti-macassars and cushions. And there would be a picture or two, a wee bit silver and a favourite text.

> We'd a row of green and blue and yellow majolica jars along the kitchen shelf for sugar, flour and meal . . . and my granny had wally dugs.

That granny also had an épèrgne and an upmarket wally close with olive-green tiles and a mahogany banister. And at that dizzy height of social prestige we can leave the surroundings of home and take a look at life within.

Affectionately recalled Edwardian and Victorian gew-gaws, bring smiles to elderly faces. But more sharply and thoughtfully remembered are the mothers and fathers, the grannies and the neighbours who peopled the tenements when many of those buildings were only quarter of a century old.

> Although in the Italian family the mother had a strong influence in the home in general the father was always the real boss. What the man said 'went'.

That was Mr. Mario Servadei's recollection of the division of power. But another rememberer, of different root-stock, saw it differently.

> My mother would always have *said* my father was head of the house, but for most of the families I ever knew that was just a myth. It was Mother ruled the roost . . . no doubt about that. No doubt at all. Mothers ruled O.K. Is that no' the way they paint it on the walls nowadays?

Mothers are best remembered for uttering precepts, cautions and bon mots, pronouncing rules, moulding morals and dispensing justice; for small thrifts and for their own constant busyness. That last she urged on all her offspring. Lily Balarsky recalls a saying of her mother's.

It was Yiddish and it came out like 'geret and geton'. It means just what it sounds like, 'get up and get on' with it. But it's Yiddish right-enough and she meant it.

Most mothers had taboos on certain words, quite outwith your actual swear words.

I never heard a swear-word in our house. That would've prostrated my Ma. But forbye them, she didn't like 'pal' or 'shut up' . . . and just about worst of all she couldnae thole 'bored' . . .

which sentiment meant much the same as 'gerup and geton'.

And there were hospitality rites that mothers followed rigorously . . . not only to have the kettle on the boil for tea and buns on the plate . . .

One of my mother's wee things, she always put a coal on the fire when someone called . . . for a kind of welcome. 'make yourself comfortable, hen', it meant. She did that whether the fire was needin' built up or no'.

If you'd eighteen shillings a week or less coming in, 'waste' was as bad a word, as much of a blasphemy, as 'pal' or 'bored'. Thrift was the eleventh commandment and if a Glasgow mother at the turn of the century had had the rearing of Moses it would have been higher on the list than some of the others.

When you were parin' potatoes my Ma used to say that if they werenae the exact same shape when you'd done then you'd taken off too thick a peelin'

And the whole population, it seemed, saved string.

We'd always to take the knots out of string then tie it in a wee bow. Ma used to scrape the butter paper like daft too. Mind you, I still do that. But you never see string now and there's no' a lot you can do wi' used sellotape.

But string was the thing.

Never a bit of string got thrown away in our house. It got all unfankled, tied round your finger and put away in the tin with Queen Victoria on it. My mother scraped egg shells too, to get out the last of the white.

There were limits to frugality though, even with eggs. Jimmy
Dewar's mother was not interested in the treasures he brought
home from the burnside at Auldhouse, would-be countrywoman
though she was.

> I found duck eggs there once and brought them home, very pleased
> with myself that we'd get them for our tea. But she'd have none of
> that. 'Duck eggs from the Auld Burn . . . no thank you!'

Home baking was another economic skill in a day when 'bought'
cakes were a mark of decadence as bad as 'bought' jam.

> My mother baked a lot on the girdle and the flat plate that hooked on
> in front of the fire for bannocks or oatcakes.

The same mother had other frugal ways.

> She'd done mill'nry and ever'thing . . . bought a hat shape and trimmed
> it up the way she wanted.

'Turning' collars and cuffs to revive shirts was also a chore in
careful homes, although some 'turners' were more dedicated and
ambitious than others. The mother-figures in Mrs. Bunty Angles'
life were her grandmother and her aunt.

> They turned all our clothes. My aunt would even turn a jacket or coat
> . . . unpick it all and make it up the other way round. She even made
> a suit for my uncle by taking an older one to pieces for a pattern to
> cut the new one from. And then she turned the old one and so she
> got two new suits.

Mealtime in most homes, when the day's doings were gone
over and the projects for the next day were vetted by a vigilant
mother, was the scene of much upbringing. Clipings by neighbours or siblings, for cheek, misdemeanours or small deceits,
might merit a cuff round the ears or an angry scolding. Mario
Servadei never forgets a Tuscany raging he once had for a minor
act of vandalism.

> I had a new penknife and I cut a tiny wee square of wood from the edge
> of the polished banister and by jove I didn't half get a hammering for
> that.

And along with the tea-time boiled eggs and jam-pieces, there was a stream of things to heed about proper conduct . . . carrying Mrs. Scobie's shopping, or Mrs. Kelly's ash-can, not speaking till you were spoken to, giving up your seat in the tramcar . . . and all the multifarious conditioning that would surely someday produce the true lady or gentleman.

Then there were Grandmothers. Apart from the Babushkas left behind in Russia or the Nonnas in Italy, grandmothers were, for the most part, either in situ or just round the corner. Paternal grannies* (the ones you *can* shove off the 'bus) were less in evidence.

> My father's mother wasn't there as often, but then she lived with her daughter's family and she mostly had to do with them.

But the *mammies'* mammies were often just another pair of hands knitting, cooking, cuffing, alternately with mothers'. And grannies were often the occupiers of the kitchen bed.

> I always got to sleep in the inshot bed wi' my granny on a Friday night and she used to give me a scone and syrup when she got up in the morning. She knitted all the time for us, my granny did . . . and she learnt me all the wee sayings about 'putting your hand to the plough' and 'Oh what a tangled web we weave . . .' and about 'two blacks not makin' a white'.

That grandmother was a home fitment, but there was another one perhaps even more firmly rooted.

> My granny kep' her winding-sheet under the bed.

However thirled to a particular house a family may have been, the day could come when there had to be a flitting. Lily Balarsky came to Glasgow from Cumnock.

> There was no Jewish community there, so we moved to Glasgow to get mixing with our own people. I remember arriving along with the furniture at the close in Stockwell Street near the old Metropole. We

---

*Ref. the immortal 'pome' . . .
  'You canny shove yer granny aff the 'bus,
  No, you canny shove yer granny
  (for she's your mammy's mammy),
  No, you canny shove yer granny aff the 'bus'.

went up to a house with a big-big hall, a huge kitchen and a room that was always called the Big Room. There was a bedroom too and we'd two concealed beds. No bathroom. Six of us were brought up there.

Eileen Reilly recalls the day when her parents had at last saved enough to bribe their way into a proper house, from their lodgings.

It was in Tollcross Road and we'd to take it furnished. That just meant a table and chairs. I was still at the stage of being carried and I was taken into this new house. It was evening and the gas was lit (I can still smell the smell of these mantles). Anyway there was a rocking chair and my father just plonked me into it, thinking it would be a great experience, but I was terrified when this thing *moved* in the half-dark with me sitting in it.

Sometimes the flitting was a team effort.

If it was maybe just round the corner you hired a horse and cart. Big flitting-vans were for 'bought' houses. (Unlike cakes or jam, 'bought' houses were infinitely desirable . . . an unlikely dream for most worthies of tenement land). Well, you'd this horse and cart, and all the neighbours helped. A flitting was rare if it was good weather. And you got tea and buns after. Or maybe fish suppers.

Neighbours, of course, were almost part of the extended family.

If you were wee and doing something wrong, the slap you got was just as likely to come from Mrs. Ferrie across the landing as from your Ma.

There were bonuses as well as clouts.

I didn't like my mother's soup, but I would take Mrs. Grove's soup from up the stair. And Arthur Grove wouldn't take his mother's tart or dumplings, so he got those from my mother.

Mrs. Duffy's tarts and Mrs. Grove's soup being interchangeable was no more odd than an Eve's pudding swopped for a special brew of coffee or the potato scones and marmalade that changed hands up and down the closes.

It's hard to see in the lonely, dreary close-entries of the 1990s, rushed through by hard-pressed couples dashing out to work, the scoured and prim places that were once the pride of each clachan of neighbours in the tenements of long ago.

We'd all to take our turn of washing the close, and Mistress Rodden up the stair always done kinda daisy-chains up ours wi' her pipe-clay . . . nothin' as common as zig-zags or squiggles. Lovely, they were.

It was squiggles though, in Pollokshaws.

. . . wee pipe-clay squiggles all up the edges.

But daisies or squiggles, the pipe-clay had its snags if the sweep of the artist's hand ranged too near the centre of the passage-way.

It got all tramped through on to your good congoleum or your rugs.

Sometimes it was the footsteps that strayed on to the pipe-clay.

The women up our close worked hard and I suppose so did the men at their jobs. But no matter how short the money was for the wives, there was always enough for the men to get their drink on a Saturday . . . and maybe more'n one. We'd two in our close; real respectable men all week . . . then stotious at the week-end, staggering up the stair singin'.

And Jack Roche remembers Dougie up their close who was musical too.

He was a big teuchter that played the pipes, and when he'd had a dram you used to get the heedrum-hodrums all night from his chanter.

There were other intriguing characters who made up the cast of the long-running soap operas of the tenements.

I mind we'd an old couple above us. The wife called her man 'auld Brodie' and he called her 'auld Biddy'.

And Peggy Carson recalls others.

When you talk about flitting what comes to my mind is no' *flitting* but *fletting*. We'd four spinster ladies next door us. Quite perjink they were . . . wore hats and gloves and everything, but we used to see them flettin' their tea. D'you know what that is? It's pourin' it into your saucer to drink. My mother gave us a roastin' for laughing at them. She made excuses . . . said it was because they were 'country'.

Cosy warrens of neighbourliness, warmth and polished brass . . . or were they?

Och, it all sounds that couthy and good when you look back . . .
close-knit communities . . . you see it all rosy. But a lot of it was
cold and uncomfortable with long working days, or worse, times
that th'was no work at all . . . frightening when you didn't have
much money. Th'was quite a lot of illnesses too, chests an'that . . .
T.B. . . . and no' much colour. Your granny was aye in black. I never
mind her any other way. And she wouldnae be out of her forties when
I knew her. Th'was bad smells too and a lot of drunkenness. A thing
I couldnae thole was comin' in from the school and wet clo'es hangin'
over the table from the pulley, slappin' your face and puttin' a damp
kind of smell over your teas. Blankets was the worst.

But the rosy haze persists, and whether it covers darker or more
sinister truths, for most of the children who ventured out from
them, the tenements are remembered as nourishing wombs that
delivered them safe and strong into the demanding life of their
city. The endless round of chores to make it so, and the sharing
out of those, will keep for another chapter.

4

Blue Sparks in the Night

Ask a Glasgow ancient about the streets of his childhood and he'll give you buskers and beggers, horses, theatre-queues and vendors, push-barrows, polis-men and pick-pockets. But above, beyond and before every other sight and sound, he'll tell you about the tramcar.

By the 1840s the early waves of immigrants to Glasgow from the countryside were dying out and it had become something of a puzzle to many a Glasgow working man (whose crofting or shepherding grandsires had thought nothing of a ten or twelve mile tramp over the hills and glens of the north-west) how he was to cover the mile or so from his tenement home to the factory where he earned his weekly living. Maybe the sight of his betters bowling genteelly along the wide city streets in carriages, to business-type occupations a lot less fatiguing, gave him a simmering staw at having to tramp the pavements to his own home on Shank's pony after the sweat of ten or more hours ill-paid labour . . . a staw that prompted action in high places. Whether there was a philanthropic move to see your ordinary bunnet-and-breeks man supplied with wheels like his master, or just money-in-it for a sharp entrepreneur, public transport, run privately, came to Glasgow streets and bridges long before the earliest recollections for these pages. First there were the little one-horse two-wheel 'noddie' 'buses for hire in the city centre; and then, by mid-19th century, longer-distance omnibuses that clip-clopped their way to suburbs like Partick and Dennistoun.

In the public mind 'bus and tram are seen so much as two distinct and separate inventions, that only a solitary 88-year-old thought to mention that the tram arrived on the scene simply as an improved 'bus.

My faither used to tell us how the first horse-buses were that slow and shoogly when he was a boy that they put down the tram-lines so's they'd be quicker and more comf'table. The rails was new but they just kinda called the buses 'tramcars'.

All the same, whether bus and tram were separate brainwaves or a progression one on the other, it was the tramcar that caught the public imagination and has lingered in Glasgow as the focus of its most nostalgic folk history . . . from the horse-drawn primitive to streamlined Empire Exhibition model and beyond.

Few now have firsthand memories of horse-powered trams but one sharp 91-year-old who spent his youth in Tollcross could just recall their last days at the end of last century.

They were dark, dirty wee things, but what I mind best was being surprised how the horses could keep going right, between the rails, and no' pull the car out the grooves. And they were just one deck of course.

But then the 'electric' came and Glasgow's love affair with its tramcars really began.

Oh aye, I got taken on one for my sixth or seventh birthday, I don't just mind which. But och, it was like the Space Age in the electric double-decker.

It was a real Glasgow thing the open-top tramcar. When you were wee you always had to go upstairs . . . summer or winter, cold or hot. And if it rained, even quite hard, well you'd always your brolly.

And the daintiest of 1991 ladies smiles at the vision . . .

Och, we were tough, were we not just tough?

By now it was the Corporation who ran the tramway services and it did its meagre best to meet the weather hazards.

On wet days right-enough, they put straw on the top deck floor.

At first the bird's-eye view of Glasgow going about its business was novelty enough, but gradually knacks of swinging aboard by the brass pole, swaying with the lurch and well-balanced strap-hanging, created a tram riding expertise as skilled in its way as those of the gentry lightly flicking a rein and prancing proudly along in its carriages. The man–in–the–street soon knew all there was to know about getting the best out of his own transport system.

At the place where yon trolley-bit joined the top deck there used to be a light when it was dark . . . a very bright light, maybe about ten inches high, and you always tried to sit ahead of that, because if you sat behind it the glare on your eyes was terrible. So it was always up the stair and out to the front.

Perhaps city streets were brighter than early fading sepia photographs suggest. Maybe the ladies did rejoice in purples and scarlets, and gay flowered hats and the men sport dashing waistcoats, but there in no doubt that the arrival of the trams, boldly banded in greens and yellows, reds and blues, according to route, brought new colour to its streets. Mrs. Lily Joseph still sees her local ones as if it was only yesterday they had trundled the rails across the Stockwell and Jamaica Bridges and out to the east end.

> Different colours for different places, yes yes. A yellow one went along Norfolk Street to Bridgeton Cross from Paisley Road and the other way was the white one from Mosspark to the University.

Mrs. Mysie Kyle is something of a tram colour historian, chanting the routes like a spelling list.

> The red car went from Millerston round by Giffnock to the Rouken Glen and back out to Bishopbriggs. The other way it was up Parliamentary Road by Monkland Street. I knew all the trams . . . the red to Riddrie, the yellow one along Nelson Street, white from Dumbreck to the University.

And with the 'blue' to the Normal School, the 'green' to the east end, the yellow along Allison Street, folk made their colour-coded way from the city-centre grid to all points of the compass.

There were even pioneers who went further afield, in *alien* trams. Miss Janet Kay explored the Lanarkshire version.

> We used to visit 'family' out in Stonehouse and I remember during a train strike we'd to take a Glasgow tram to Cambuslang, get the Lanarkshire tram to Hamilton, change there for one to Lanark and walk the rest of the road to Stonehouse. Same coming back, the other way round.

You could get a cheap family outing too, by tramcar. Struan Yule remembers one favourite trip with his grandfather.

> It was the yellow tram that came our way and went on out to Riddrie, and Grandad used to take me and my brother on that, and then on a kind of safari along footpaths to find the place where William Wallace was betrayed to the English by Sir John Menteith. There was a well and a farmhouse and my grandad was sure it was the very place where Wallace was taken. I can see him yet knocking on the door to ask, and not getting a very certain answer.

And Jimmy Dewar recalls days out to the far end of Barrhead with his mother.

We got off there and walked up by Crosstobs, through a gate up to the Gleniffer Braes for a picnic. Mother was a great one for the fresh air up the braes. But there was another real bargain of a trip when we were wee. You could go anywhere on a children's penny ticket right through the summer . . . from terminus to terminus . . . say from Renfrew to Auchenshuggle . . . or was it maybe Airdrie? Anyway, it was halfway across Scotland that, for a penny! We used to go to Renfrew Ferry and there was a café there that we got ginger beer and watched the ships going up and down.

Nearer home, city centre weans packed the red 'caurs' bound for Rouken Glen and it was claimed that they brought fifteen thousand people to the park every bright summer week-end and made the terminus there as busy as Glasgow Cross on a Saturday.

The system brought with it other interesting fixtures besides rails and overhead cables.

The bundy clocks . . . d'you mind the bundy clocks? I liked it when I was wee and the driver timed in at the bundy at the side of the street.

If a driver wasn't up to time there it was perhaps because there were queues further back along the route at the tram stops.

They were quite neat, fancy wee things, the tram stops. Half green and half red, and they kind of bulged into rims at the bottom. Some just said TRAM STOP in white lettering, other ones had FARE STAGE or CARS STOP HERE IF REQUIRED. I's'pose they could just go scooshing past those ones if there was no one waiting to get on or off.

When dozens of cars were shuttling and plying in procession between termini in all directions it was inevitable that there were mishaps. Mrs. Agnes Grove remembers . . .

Sometimes in frosty weather the trams used to jump the points and the driver had to take them back a bit and try again. They'd long metal cleek things to shift the points, that they kept in the driver's wee cubby at the front end of the car.

Mrs. Mysie Kyle too recalls the hazard of bad weather.

I remember the winter of 1939/40 when the snow was deep and they'd to keep the tramlines clear and cut paths out to the rails from the tram stops.

And John Adamson . . .

> I've always mind of one stormy winter, maybe in the 'twenties, seeing a tramcar blown over on its side on yon chuckie track alongside the Mosspark Boulevard.

Jimmy Dewar recalls a type of mishap that was recurrent at his local terminus.

> After I saw it the first time I was always a bit scared when the trams came up past the Vicky Infirmary, because at the monument yonder where the rails stopped short a tram would overshoot sometimes and get de-railed. Then a trailer had to come out from the depot to drag it back again.

But if all was well at the terminus and the driver and conductor had a tasty ham or cheese piece, they sometimes farmed out one of their duties to eager volunteers.

> I remember the trams came down Sinclair Drive and they'd to change the trolley round there, so you used to wait for them and get them to let you pull the trolley off the cable, walk round and hitch it back on again the other way. That was a great thing to get to do. It was a single bar trolley and you pulled it down on a spring. If th'were nice drivers they let you do that.

Those favoured boys, though, wouldn't be the ones caught taking free hurls hanging on to the brass platform-pole when the conductor was aloft punching his tickets.

> Yous could get yersel' a mile or two through the toon for nothin' that way . . . jumpin' on two or three different cars until yous got chased or clouted by one of the conductors.

But conductors and clippies weren't always simply chasers, clouters or handers-out of coveted chores. They were legendary for repartee and apochryphal stories. Eileen Reilly remembers.

> There was a conductor who did our route and in those days they called out the name of each fare stage (y'know, the stop where the fare went up by a ha'penny). They'd shout Sauchiehall Street! Argyle Street! Cook Street! . . . Well, on our route he used to shout out 'Gor-bals . . . Wee Jerusalem!

The last night of the trams in Glasgow is talked of with all the enthusiasm of the last night of the proms, with overtones of *Rule Britannia* and *Land of Hope and Glory*.

It was sad. I was in Argyle Street when the last one went along to Auchenshuggle. I was near greetin'. Maybe I *was* greetin'.

Bundies, wee red boxes for uncollected fares, the clatter of the destination blind being changed at the terminus, the rhythmic sideways sway of the conductor swinging over seat backs for the turn-round, the touches of stained glass at window tops, the slow death of the colour swathes to the uniform green and yellow of the 'new' trams, . . . the clippies, the blue sparks in the night, the ping of the ticket punch, the platform bell and the big brass driver's handle . . . There's not a rememberer but mourns them all.

Next to their beloved tramcars, ripe Glasgow people best remember the horses that clopped the streets of an older day . . . from high-stepping aristocrats and spanking trap ponies to weary little nags that pulled slow cadging-carts along the gutter.

The first city suburbs rose as fine honey-stoned, ashlar mansions and villas, within a lunch-time's drive away from the professional and merchant classes' places of business. Pollokshields, Newlands, Hillhead and the far reaches of Great Western Road became the places for solid citizens to be, and it was to and from the gracious avenues of des. res. there, that carriages rolled four times a day, horses and vehicles gleaming, like Porsche or B.M.W. every inch the status symbol of their day.

When my Ma was fourteen she came from near Oban to go into service as a housemaid in a big place in Pollokshields. Th'was a cook forbye, and a woman for the rough work. And th'was a coachman that did the garden and kept the carriage nice, and groomed the horses . . . rubbed up the leather and brasses an' that. He took his gentleman (that was a lawyer, I think) into his office in the town, then went back for him, dinner and teatime. My mother married the coachman and they took a wee grocery after that, but he used to tell me about the kind of procession of carriages that went in and out, all competin' wi' each other to be the best turn-out. I think he always wished he was still a coachman.

Mrs. Millicent Davies remembers a house in Roman Road, Bearsden . . . with *two* horses.

> The man who built the Highland Railway lived there and they kept a carriage and pair.

For those minor gentry who fancied something more of the 'country' life there were villages like Busby and Milngavie where they could live and be driven to the local railway station to catch the business train.

> The office-boys took the early train, then the clerks a wee bit after that. And then there was a later train for the gents from the big villas who were the bosses. They came in their carriages and stepped up into the late train from wee boxes the guard or the coachman put down for them.

So it was all very spick and span and 'white glove', but Mrs. Nell Dinsmor remembers another inevitable side of the carriage-and-pair days and what it was like to live next-door to where the sweating horses came home at night.

> See that wall down there? Well, beside it yonder was the dung midden for the horses that were kept in the stable there.

But it wasn't only fine carriage horses that were loved and cosseted by their owners and grooms. The plain cuddies who were partners with their masters in earning a family living were cherished with perhaps even greater affection . . . by Ann Hutchison for one, looking back to faraway childhood.

> When I was wee in Pollokshaws there was lots of horses and carts. My Daddy had a lovely horse. We used to stable her at Brown and Adams works and then down beside the chapel. He'd a real nice cart too. Nancy was an awful nice horse. We loved her and d'you know this? On Saturday mornings Nancy used to come right down the hill and up the front steps of the house (it was a main door house) to get a treacle piece . . . right up the steps! Just herself!. Fancy her comin' down all that way from the chapel for that treacle piece. And she brought the cart with her! My Daddy would come following her, but away behind. She got oats an' that every day right-enough, but she liked her treacle piece.

Even when the Dobbins weren't petted, home-stabled members of the family, just the memory of them raising sparks on the streets of the city of their youth brings a smile to all who speak about them. Coal carts, delivery carts, builders' carts and their horses were all part of the passing show, steamy, sometimes scruffy and overworked, sometimes proud and easy, always passing steadily on their way. But it's the vending carts, stopping and starting, progressing only a few yards at a time, that became real friends . . . the Betsys, the Dapples, the Daisies. Struan Yule recalls their like.

> When I was young in Dennistoun, the streets were alive with carts and vendors and I remember one pony-drawn float that went up and down the different streets with a husband and wife selling fruit. Sometimes a tenement window, maybe three floors up would be thrown open and a housewife would call down for the man to bring up potatoes, apples, pears or whatever. It was the husband did the calling of the wares too. 'Fine Can-ary bi-na-nas the day, shill'n the duzz-in'

There was another hawker that sold tripe from barrels draped with white towels and, if you could tell the difference between tripe and towels, and were interested, then the cry,

> 'Bags, sheepsh' bags, sheepsh' bags' . . .

would have you hurrying down for a yard or so for your tea. And maybe you would wait on the soor-dook cart to get some of that to slake down the tripe, as someone else recalls.

> There was a soor-dook cart went round the streets near us. My mother loved soor-dook and she used to send us out to get it to drink fresh with the wee globs of butter floating in it. You took out a jug to the wee tap at the back of the cart. It was great . . . cool and fresh . . . funny that, soor-dook being fresh . . . but it was.

Other nights it was fish for tea.

> There was Ovens the fish man came to the Wellmeadow with his cart and his handbell. We bought fish off him.

No mention of whether it was whiting or cod, but elsewhere, down Cathcart Road, the soor-dook went with salted herrings.

> Fridays we'd salted herrin's off of Haddie Joe's cart. That made you thirsty and you waited wi' your can for the soor-dook man to come along.

If the soor–dook cart failed you, there were other ways of cooling down, that Mrs. Lily Joseph remembers from a lifetime ago in the Gorbals.

> When you were wee you used to see water-carts spreading water over the streets. There was a barrel on them with a pipe at the back and the water came out that stroup. Sometimes they stopped it when you went by but if you were cheeky and shouted a wee rhyme at the man . . .
> 'Mind oot, mind oot
> Here comes the water scoot',
> then he'd put it on that-heavy you got all wet. Did that for fun, so he did.

The real kings among the horses were the big draught-horses. Mrs. Agnes Grove and others remember them trudging up the High Street, but those whose beat was nearer the city centre are the ones best recalled.

> I remember the draught-horses pulling carts up West Nile Street. Part of that street was wooden causeys at one time . . . very quiet . . . but at the time I remember it was the ordinary cobbles with two smooth tracks for the cart wheels to run up. The boys that waited in the street to help with the horses used to put on a kind of galoshes over their feet to run out to lead them up or push them.

To most, the sight of the plunging horses was of passing if awe-inspiring interest . . . a bonus to the day. But there was one child who made formal visits, on purpose to see them . . . and even took calling gifts.

> I always loved horses and used to like to go and watch the trace-horses in West Nile Street. I loved the scene there as a little girl. There would be three or four of them at the foot of the hill, and wee boys sitting on the kerb. Then a heavy load on a cart would come along and one, or maybe two would run out and hitch the nice big fresh horse on to the front. The original horse would still be in the shafts. I used to fancy that when he felt the new horse taking the weight to tow him he would just say 'Right chap, it's your turn, you get on with it'. And the boy would lead them up between the two smooth tracks to the top of the hill. They'd get unhitched there and the boy would lead the trace-horse down by the gutter and take his place in the queue of wee lads to lead

the next load up. It was like The Grand Old Duke of York, or maybe
pilots on the river. These boys were very popular, a great street sight.
And y'know they used to be given their own party at Christmas.

A little yearly largesse perhaps on an otherwise sparse livelihood.
This affection for horses was no childhood whim of the small
visitor, for she goes on,

> . . . even when I was older I never went into town without going round
> to see my horses, and I never went without sugar lumps. I *knew* the
> horses . . . intimately! There was one that had been through the First
> War and got wounded. He'd a great long scar along his side . . . about
> ten inches. A real old war-horse. And he knew *me*. I took toffees for
> the boys too.

Those recalled wooden causeys had been laid to keep horses from
slipping, but the idea didn't take on and was never widespread.
Instead there were private do-gooders known in their communities
for being ready for emergencies. Mrs. Mysie Kyle's mother was
one of those up Garngad Hill.

> In those days they didn't salt or grit the streets. But because my parents
> had their factory, their lemonade and toffee to make, my mother had a
> fire going summer and winter, and she used to save all her ashes to put
> out on the street for the horses when the frost came and it was slippy.

But wooden cobbles, ashes or careful driving couldn't always
prevent accident and one of the real street spectacles of the days
of the horse was 'the fallen horse'.

> There was this sort of uneven clatter told you a horse was down and
> was thrashing about trying to get up. It used to get all wild-eyed and
> sweaty . . . all trim'ly y'know.

And when that happened, in Garngad at least, they knew where
to call for help, and ashes were soon being rushed out from the
lemonade factory.

> My father would always be right out there with the fire ashes when
> a horse went down, they threw the ashes all round it, then took the
> belly-band off, took the horse out the trams and pulled them away.
> There was always a big crowd and they got them yelling as loud as they
> could to give the horse a right good fright and made it scramble up on its

feet by getting a grip on the ashes. You couldnae let it lie there you see.
My father used to say if it wasn't up in ten minutes it was done for.

Others used sacks instead of ashes, and drummed some passing
boy into service to sit on the horse's head, the most frequently
remembered procedure for pacifying animals and getting them
to their feet without frenzy. One such passing boy was Mr. Jack
Roche now aged eighty-nine.

I mind once in Monteith Row a horse'd slipped and fell, coupin' the cab
on its side . . . and here a gent grabs me and makes me sit on the beast's
heid while they unhitched it. Me, I was terrified, but I done it and after
it was up and slitherin' into its trams, he gie'd me a florin . . . a florin!
After that I'd of sat on a tiger's heid, nae bother.

There's more to Glasgow street scenes remembered than tramcars and horses, but for the time being we'll run the 'caurs' into the
depot and see the horses into their stabling for a rest and maybe a
check-up on their street-worn shoes.

The Cartcraigs Co-operative stables were just down the Barrhead Road
from the Round Toll, with the smiddy beside them. It was a great thing
when we were young to go down at tea-time and see the horses getting
led in there.

Another such sanctuary was at Muirend.

Long before there was the Toledo cinema there was the old Bogton
farmhouse that's fields went away up to Netherlee thonder. The cows
came in mornin' and night for milkin'. There was horses too. Some
were just for people learnin' to ride and they'd other ones for pulling
the milk floats.

With all but the late-night trams in the depots and the horses bedded
down for the night we can close the book for a moment on city
streets and open it in a later chapter to look at their landmarks and
some of the citizens who knew them.

5

Hets and Peevers and Kick the Can

There's a deep-rooted belief among those who played their games eighty or more years ago in nearly empty streets and wide back-courts, that today's young have neither the gift for play nor the imagination, the adventure and the fun they themselves had in their green years. They've gone soft, say the elderly, with television 'pap' and 'little ponies' sporting fluorescent hair.

Perhaps tight budgets, and the environment of their echoing closes and tightly defined territories shaped and refined their games in older days. But it may not be so different now. Perhaps imagination is still stimulated and skills are still honed, although by other surroundings and a kind of sophisticated gear unknown in the past.

These pages though, are not about the precocious weans of today who can slot in videos, operate computers, flicking the right switches before they can handle a knife and fork. They are about how their grannies and grandpas jumped and chanted and spun their peeries long long ago.

There's a hint of the part played by environment and the 'available', in an observant memory of Jenny Logan's.

When I was very small we lived in Dennistoun and I played peever there . . . and ball beds. But then we moved out to the suburbs where the pavements were just rough ash . . . the playground was too, so you couldn't draw chalk-beds for those games. I missed my peever and ball-beds.

Another who had to adapt to new ways was Jimmy Dewar.

When I left Battlefield for Pollokshaws I found everything was different . . . different ways of playing things, they talked different, different words and accents. Some of them were a bit rougher maybe. But it was good. It was lively and there was lots to do . . . places to go . . . more countryside.

To Ann Hutchison, Pollokshaws was not new territory to explore, but her home stamping-ground from birth.

There was nowhere like it. We'd skipping and peever and ball and that. And everyb'dy was close. If your mother was out, or if she was ill, you just went next door and played there.

One of her neighbours had a wryer idea of the closeness . . .

. . . an' if you were cheeky or wild or that, someb'dy else's Ma went her dinger at you and handed you a clout you wouldnae forget in a hurry. And in them days you didnae go whining and cliping, for fear of getting a harder one at home.

That was maybe a wee digression from pragmatic choices of what to play at next. So back to the lively kee-hoys and crazes among the tenements and let the Jennies and Jimmies get on with their new customs in suburbia.

There may have been recurring patterns in the play but the young did not detect them themselves. Struan Yule . . .

. . . your playing went by seasons . . . just crazes that came up, you never knew how . . . one day it was Moshie, then the next you were into a fortnight of Kick-the-Can.

But apart from those games with rules, there was what you might call just 'play' . . . opportunist ploys dependent on passing traffic and people or on a serendipitous find. Even the weather, wet or dry.

You could easy play on the streets then. There wasn't that much traffic. They were cleaner too, the streets . . . wi' the men hosin' them down in the middle of the night. And th'was horse-drawn watering-carts too when it was hot weather, and us boys used to follow them wi' bare feet. They'd sprinkler-bars at the back and you used to could dance your way along behind, gettin' your feet nice'n cool.

If, on the other hand, there was rain instead of sun, you just literally changed your tack.

> We used to make paper boats and race them down the gutter after a good plump of rain.

Rain provided entertainment for Alex Donnelly too.

> My father had his wee pipe-clay work up a kind of close, and on wet days we used to get wee bits of kind of dry clay, go up t'the landing above the street and sprinkle it on the top of umbrellas to dissolve and run down.

Just such a vantage point above passers-by provided diversion for another rememberer too.

> There were men from a pipe-band came down the street sometimes when we were wee, and I remember crouching on the high shed roof above them and dropping wee stones picked out the rough-cast, down into their busbies.

Alex Donnelly had another perch too.

> Sometimes we used to climb on the railings outside the pub to listen to the men singing.

But when he's asked, 'Was your father a singer, is that where you get your music?'

> Naw, naw. Never heard him singing but in the pub.

There were back-court romps and illicit hurls on tramcar platforms or the backs of carts. These were common to all areas where there were streets, back-greens or tram routes. But there were also venue features of particular districts that held fascination for playing. Lily Balarsky ran her tigs as one of a long line of weans who for centuries have pranced about on Glasgow Green.

> We used to play round yon nice fountain near the gate opposite the law-courts . . . played tig and release and all that.

Another rememberer risked life and limb, or a good head-bashing on a small rail-line near his home.

I was one of the last that used to play on the lime buggies that ran
to kilns up our way, and then down again. Then the lime-pits was
done and the buggies stopped, so th'was no more of that. But th'was
coal-trucks too that we played on, that ran to the station. You'd to
mind out for the *man* though. If you got caught he'd gie you a cuff,
or maybe threaten to get the polis. They werenae safe them buggies.
The man was quite right.

Do they still make fires on cold days, and bake potatoes in the
embers, then bite in to savour the faint electric shock on their
tongues from the charred skins? Or have the satisfying dangers of
that been abolished along with the sensible taking-over of bonfires
and squibs by the Establishment?

A less hazardous but equally interesting way to pass the time
was occasionally offered to lucky small boys with a providential
find almost on their own doorstep. One, living next door to the
local synagogue, had the joy, after there had been a party there, of
draining the lemonade bottles from the crate put out for collection
the morning after.

More structured games to be played properly, required a *group* of
youngsters and also counting-out preliminaries. 'Azeentie-teentie'
had several versions depending on whether you learned one of the
bawdy or one of the genteel rhymes.

> Azeentie-teentie figgary fell
> Ell dell dominell
> Urky purky taury rope
> An tan toosie Jock
> You . . . are . . . out!

That was alright. That was 'nice'. But the street-wise had another
version that began . . .

> Azeentie-teentie haligolum
> Pitchin' totties up the lum . . .

No one cared to finish that, for fear of what rhymed with 'lum', but
there was a local variation chanted out happily, that was peculiar to
the area round Todd Street.

> Azeentie-teentie haligolum
> The cat went out to get some fun
> It got some fun in Toddy's grun'
> Azeentie-teentie haligolum.

Another incomprehensible ditty, reeled off to find a 'het' is recalled by Eileen Reilly.

> Chinese government, black man's *daugh*-ter
> Tra la la it's a very fine day
> The wind blows high, down from the sky
> And out goes Biddy with a big black eye . . .

. . . and the players circled round the counter-out, whose eyes were shut until, on the last word, she pointed to the Molly or the Biddy who was to be 'het'. Peggy Carson recalls another . . .

> . . . in the days when little Black Sambo was your friend and not your racial thing, there was Eenie-meenie-manny-mo. And I mind of Eevy-neevy-nick-nack.

Whatever the rhyme, the object was to find the one that would be catcher chaser or seeker. Simple 'het' games depended on nothing but three or four children at a loose end. There was Leave-O with chaser and chased, and a den that no self-respecting catcher 'mooched' for fear of the mocking chant . . . 'You're moochin' the den, you big fat hen!' And played universally among the closes was Robinson Crusoe. Bunty Angles and Eileen Reilly speak for over forty rememberers.

> Oh, you played Robinson Crusoe up and down all the closes, with the one that was 'het' away hiding somewhere in one of them. It was really scarey.
>   It was eerie when you played near tea-time in winter . . . the calling up and down the closes in the gaslight. The one that was 'het' ran away into an entry (maybe up to the stair-heid or down to the dunny) with the rest shouting
>   Robinson Crusoe, give us a call,
>   Give us an answer or naethin' at all!
> He would answer in a wee squeaky voice or a gruff-gruff one and they'd try and guess where he was and catch him before he ran back to the den.

For the girls there were 'statues', douce and lady-like for some, flamboyant and dramatic for the actresses among them. It was served by a low wall or, even better, the school-shed bench.

> Maybe five or six stood on the shed seat and the one that was 'het' gave her hand to each of the others and whirled them one by one down to the floor. They'd to stand stock still in whatever position they landed. Then she chose the best statue for the next whirler. If you moved or giggled you didn't get a shot at being 'het'.

Then there were roaming chains with sturdy leaders dislocating their shoulders to yank screaming enders off their feet. And there were all the versions of what one octogenarian called 'Hiding'-seek. Hiding-seek, Kee-hoy or High-spy . . . whatever they called it, if there was a tin can to be found, there was a new dimension that turned it all into High-spy-kick-the-can.

> I suppose right enough it was really *I*-spy, but in Glasgow we all called it *High*-spy. You done it just the same, except the first back to the den kicked the can, and got being the next 'het'.
>
> Th'were other games that you used *things* in . . . balls like. You stotted them against the wall and done wee complicated things between each stot, clapping your hands or twirling round. That was clappie or twirlie. Then you lifted your leg over it. Y'did all these things till you fumbled the ball. Then if you were just by yourself you began again, if not then it was someb'dy else's turn. Th'were wee rhymes too, to keep up the beat. I was stotting balls in the thirties and th'was one went . . .
>
> Who's that walking down the street?
> Miss-is Simpson on her feet.
> She's been marr-ied twice't be-fore
> Now she's chapping on *Ed-ward*'s door.

Skipping ropes in their season rocked and cawed and snaked under twinkling feet, to a dozen jingles.

> There was one . . . you skipped a few yourself, then you chanted,
>   'I call in my sis-ter Ka-ty'
> and she'd to jink under the rope and in to jump along with you.

Eileen Reilly remembers 'French' ropes.

> You'd two enders with two ropes and you cawed them opposite ways. That was tricky. And then 'Belgium ropes' (sic). In Belgium ropes you

cawed at three-times the speed, so you'd to stay up in the air over the third caw. If you got a smack with the ropes in that, you got *some* weal!

It was your mother's old clo'es line you played with and if it wasn't heavy enough you'd to pleat three lengths together. Och, and your modesty went when you played ropes. You wrapped your skirt round your thighs and pulled your knickers over the top.

Peggy Carson . . .

Swinging the rope in a low snake was called 'wavy', and it was just for weans. 'High-low water' was kid stuff too! *It* was lifting the rope up a wee bit at a time, to jump over . . . not cawing or anything. You could make it a bit better by turning your wilkies over it, or doing a cart-wheel.

And peevers. Only the deprived small girls who had migrated to ash pavements and fancy houses in the suburbs, were non-peeverers. Lily Balarsky is sure that all the rest had peevers of some kind even if they were only boot-polish tins.

We'd all our peevers. Mine was always a nice piece of granite. See, we lived near the Clyde and there was always big piles of chips or stones on the quayside, ballast most likely, from the boats. You got good peevers there. And these piles y'know, we used to run up and down them . . . did that a lot . . . ran up and slid down. Ruined your shoes. And we used to get chased by the watchman. I s'pose that made it more fun.

If there wasn't a quorum for anything but *solo* peever your determined player, tired of that, might use her chalk to decorate her peerie, and then flex her whip for action.

You used different colours of chalk, and you made a design on the top so's when you whipped it and the peerie spun, you got a swirl of colour. Then you could wet your finger to rub it off and do a different pattern.

To some street-wise children tops were for weans, like 'high–low water' and 'wavy', for one of the deadliest put-downs they threw at timid players in other games was,

'Stick Bubbly . . . away an' spin yer peerie'.

I mind getting tormented like that by bigger ones when I was doing my peerie. But I just took my wee whip across their legs and it wasnae me that was bubbly then.

There must have been unisex city clachans where hoops and cleeks were for everyone and sang across the paving-stones for boys and girls alike . . . but that wasn't everywhere.

Up our street they were for the boys just. Th'was only one girl that ran wi' a gird. We thought she was a daft tomboy, and just got on wi' stotting our balls.

If the girls in *his* street sniffed at cleeking the hoops, Jack Roche didn't even notice.

Oh aye, we'd all our gir's. Nob'dy had a bike and the gir' was the next best to that . . . took you everywhere . . . miles it took you. It was wild. Great.
  If your gir' got broken or the wee ring came off, you'd to get it sorted at the smiddy. First time I went there I was frightened when the water fizzed on the red-hot.

Come the summer children craiked at mothers and grannies for new marble bags, had a few practice-shots on the kitchen floor ready for real contests, and then went out to skech their bools or cley dawds across the pavement. Whatever Mario Servadei's forebears called them in Italy, he was sufficiently integrated to have 'jauries'.

Oh yes, I'd jauries all right . . . and glassies and steelies. And we'd all plunkers to flick at the marbles in a circle, a kind of kitty of them you'd to knock out for keepers.

That was 'Ringie' to some, and a form of 'Moshie' to others.

But the quickest way home from school was playing your ordinary jauries straight along the gutter. Y'know I'd a big tragedy once. There was a hole in my marble bag.

Bogies now . . . there was thrill. Even if earlier traffic wasn't the hazard it is in the 1990s when it would be unthinkable to hurl yourself down the likes of Hill Street, Millbrae or Battlefield Road on a bogie, it was nevertheless a perilous undertaking, and many a small boy scraped his boots to death, braking at the end of a one-in-eight gradient.

It was lethal, that game. And another risk was that Sergeant McTavish
would chase you, and that would be the ba' on the slates . . . till the next
time. Bogies was great!

So was doormats. Oh, there's hang-gliding and water ski-ing and
all-your-orders now, but there were risks to be run in 1905 or
1906 riding down Whitehill Street on a foot-scraper. It's Miss
Jenny Logan who remembers it now, but it was really all Tom
McCulloch's fault!

He was my friend and he brought out one of these old wire mats. He
had it on a string and I'd to sit on it while he pulled me down that hill.
I'd on a little pink dress with white silk spots, and it was all into holes
at the back with the dragging wire. My mother wasn't very pleased to
say the least, and I never did that again.

Another who wasn't content with tame girlie ploys was Christina
Rodger in Govan.

The men coming out the docks and the yard used to call me Tomboy
Rodger. I played all the wild games with the boys, footb'll and kick-
the-can . . . all that.

And who would deny her her fling . . . for there were harder times
coming.

My mother died when I was thirteen and my father was an invalid that
could just sit in his chair and tell me how to do things. I'd to leave
the school to keep things going at home. So I was a wee housewife at
thirteen. Not a schoolgirl any more.

And sadly not a tomboy either.

Let's close these pages on that glimpse of football, for Kirsty's
gone home to her household chores, and most others to do their
stint at coal-humping and the brasses. She won't often be back out
to play, but we can look forward in another chapter to a few more
gegs and pastimes that the less trauchled of her playmates were still
able to enjoy. And we can perhaps recall there an indoor game or
two that even she can join in, between seeing to her scrubbing and
cooking and clawting out the clinkers from her range fire.

6

Did you Ever Hear of a Tuppenny Hing?

Walk up Sauchiehall Street three Saturdays in a row and the buskers will have changed as many times. Break dancers will have given way to a twanging guitar or a couple of oboe students from the music college. But there's a whole tribe of more durable, kenspeckle characters remembered as having livened the streets of Glasgow in an older day . . . some busking like the tall paper-tearer outside the Cosmo Cinema or the grey-haired fiddler in Union Street, like the cloggie-dancers entertaining theatre queues. Some were simply familiar figures like the Clincher or the 'legless' beggar on Jamaica Bridge with those limbs akimbo'd out of sight under him, like the flower-seller outside the Georgic Tearoom, or Miss Cranston sweeping into one of her establishments. Those were uniques . . . recognisable, even nameable, people whose faces still linger in minds after well over half a century. But there were others, faceless as individuals perhaps, nevertheless remembered and regarded with affection as groups. Some gave the citizen a sense of security, or kept his streets clean and decent, some made him laugh or treated him to a song-for-a-penny, some by garb and habit gave a personality to Glasgow, peculiarly its own. Peggy Carson and Jimmy Dewar have clear memories of some of them.

Remember the lamplighters tramping round with their poles? I mind the wee clatter when the glass flap went up and let the end of it through . . . then the 'plop' when the light came up and the wee tinkle of the flap going down again. We used to swing on the crossbars and it was a game to see how far you could dreep forward like the long-jump they do in the Olympics.

I liked the lamplighters, and one of my favourite poems at school was,

>My tea is nearly ready,
>And the sun has left the sky,
>It's time to take the windie,
>To see Leerie going by.

That was Edinburgh right enough. But I remember them, all eerie in the dark Glasgow closes. The men had wee ladders to get up to the gas brackets in there. They lit them some different way from the pole they used in the street.

And an eavesdropper chimes in . . .

Oh-here, I thought the wee ladder was for to change a mantle or that, but I mind yon greenish kind of light falling all round the lamp-post.

The policeman and the postman lit up dark corners too.

They had lamps. They would be oil I think at the time I'm talking about, but quite bright and they shone them into doorways. The postman had a smaller, flatter lamp but oil too, I suppose.

Little Jenny Logan's mother knew the worth of another civic servant and had firm strictures for her daughter about the crossing sweeper.

When I was small and going down Whitehill Street to Duke Street for messages, there were several streets that ran across those two and Mother used to warn me not to dirty my boots but cross where the sweepers kept the junctions clear of mud and droppings that made the rest of the streets dirty and muddy.

Then with a shake of her nonagenarian head she muses,

Crossing sweepers just kind of died out . . .

. . . slipping away unnoticed like old red telephone boxes now in the 1990s, and Scots pound notes.

By the end of the Second War 'shovellers' too were a dying breed, although they had been as regular a part of the scene as the official crossing sweepers. On very busy streets horse-droppings would be ground in by trundling cartwheels and Clydesdale hooves, but at quieter stretches they were prized by dung entrepreneurs as a saleable commodity in posh suburbs with gardens and scooped up while they were still steaming and pungent. One thing sure, the drivers felt no social responsibility.

You took not a blind bit of notice if your pony did it when you were on your way to the school in the trap in the mornings. Just left it for the rain or the boys with spades. They sold it round the doors out in the posh districts.

Another part of the army of cleansers was the whole battalion of stairwomen. Thorough or slittery, they clattered their buckets up and down wally closes whose tenants were above that sort of thing themselves, but who inspected their Glasgow-Style close-tiles when the women had finished and before they handed over their coppers. Unless the job was pre-paid.

Annie was our stairwoman. She was as thin as a twig and she'd a big feather hat that wafted and waved about as she scrubbed . . . and she wore men's boots. My mother sometimes left Annie's money in the pail of water at the door ready for her, if she was going out. I suppose she and others like her thought they were quite charitable to be employing these women.

Such ladies thought quite kindly too of those they called 'shawlies', and while they may not have wanted to *be* one themselves, there's no denying that they looked on these women, their babies held firm in their tartan plaids, with sentimental affection and some respect, as a colourful feature of the city's streets. Words like 'sensible' 'warm', 'a great support for the baby', (who was slung securely in the inner fold and happed close to her like a papoose) are trotted out in patronising admiration by those whose nurses or little housemaids wheeled out *their* weans to the park in handsome baby-carriages.

> I remember my mother, who was quite an elegant lady and very conscious of her social position, being dumbfounded by a query, quite innocent, from her washing-woman as she was hanging up a travelling-rug to dry. 'Was this Patricia's and Thomas's shawl when they were wee?' Mother afternoon-tea'd out on that one for many a long year.

There were shawlie-women to be seen wherever wage pokes did not allow the buying of coats or costumes. Mrs. Mysie Kyle recalls them firmly rooted in an area not far from her old home.

> Garngad Road was the home of the shawlie-women. I've heard folk say that they often went barefoot. But I don't remember that . . . and there wouldn't have been any need for it, because there were all those sugar-bags they could wrap round their feet, or they could wear slippers.

And what self-respecting woman would go barefoot if she could sally out in a pair of Tate and Lyle's designer swaddlings?

Sometimes the shawlies did venture out of their own haunts and into those of suburban folk. They came with sheets looped into bags, to buy the ladies' old clothes for a few coppers.

> I remember Mamma standing at the door of our house in Newlands haggling with an old clothes' wife over what the woman would give her for things she had no intention of ever wearing again. And the worst of it is, I thought at the time she was quite right . . . very thrifty, a good bargainer.

It's difficult to know what those good women would actually do with the big-brimmed hats and feather-boas, or the waisted jackets and hobble skirts . . . more suitable braws surely for the Sunday noon promenades for which they had first been bought in the years of Miss Alison Dow's childhood.

> I can only just remember. I must have been about four . . . before the First War, and it would've been Great Western Road on a Sunday after church, walking along with my parents. Mamma pushed my sister in a high pram. You met a lot of people doing that Sunday stroll there, with the men lifting their hats (I'm sure some were tall hats) and the ladies kind of dipping their parasols. The young men like my uncles had boaters. Then we used to go to my Grandma's for Sunday dinner. I don't remember much about my Grandpa except that he'd a silky beard I used to stroke, and a wee silver tube of water under his lapel for the flower he always had in his button-hole.

On weekdays Mammas surrendered their prams to their Nannies and the afternoon baby walk was another familiar west-end scene.

> We lived out Sauchiehall Street and I can just about recall my Nana taking me with her when she pushed the big wicker pram with my wee brother, in the green bit in front of the crescents. Then she used to sit with other Nannies while we played. I do remember I'd a sailor suit with a big round hat and an elastic under my chin. I used to get a row for sucking that elastic and making my chin sore. I didn't like my Nana much. She used to push me by the shoulder and she sucked peppermints.

Social walking was a feature of bygone week-ends for all ages. Peggy Carson and a dozen others recall their own versions of those outings, the sight they presented, the people they met . . . or tried to meet.

> Th'were a lot of places where people just walked, on Sunday afternoons. Th'were the family stretches of road, and then the young folks had theirs . . . I'm sayin' 'just walkin" but it wasnae only that wi' the youngsters . . . och aye, th'was Victoria Road . . . Great Western Road . . . Alexandra Parade . . . even the Art Galleries was a great place for girls and fellas walkin', seein' if y'could get off . . . gettin' a 'lumber' . . . or gettin' a 'click' some of them used to call it. Didnae matter what you *called* it but. It was the same thing. I did it myself . . . Glasgow

Road or, if it was wet, the Art Galleries. But I got quite a likin' for pictures while I was at it there, and that never left me.

So the human scene in Glasgow shifts and changes and the tide of familiar figures ebbs and flows with day and night and changing season. But what of the landmarks? Each rememberer for these chapters has his or her own private trove of recollected places, some still there, others long gone. They lay to the north and south, the east and west and in the heart of the city itself. To the north young Janet Kay once walked by Glasgow's ancient stream.

> I used to walk along what had been the banks of the Molendinar to get to the Cathedral. Y'know they knocked down the old buildings in the Ladywell (och, that was sinful!). But when they did it, a part of the burn that hadn't been seen for ages, was exposed. Later on they covered it with a pipe and now I think you can maybe see a wee bit somewhere the other side of Duke Street.

And she has an odd little minding of the River Clyde too.

> When I was at Strathclyde school the river was very low at one period for some reason, from the weir to the part further up-country . . . just a mud hole really. And all the boys went out at playtime into it. What a glaury mess . . . paddling in the mud. And oh the stories that went about! You know, someone had found a diamond dagger or a Roman tool. Nothing of the kind, of course.

From the east end of the city comes a second-hand memory passed on to his grandson, the late Tom Watson, by Walter Freer the man they called Mr. Glasgow when he had the letting of its Burgh Halls early in the century . . . a memory of Freer's that puts the Great Eastern and the Portugal Street 'models' up there with the Hiltons and the Holiday Inns of the world.

> Did you ever hear of a Tuppenny Hing? It's hard to credit, but it seems when my grandfather was young, a down-and-out could go to some miserable dark cellar where there were ropes slung across, and for tuppence he could 'hing' over it with the rope under his oxters so he could get a sleep without lying on a filthy floor among others who paid nothing or maybe just a penny.

Jack Roche had heard of the 'hing' too and thought it had a later refinement.

Like what you do on the footb'll terracing I s'pose.

Such social recollections of a rougher Glasgow belong not to the fine displays at Kelvingrove or other conventional museums but in the startling exhibitions of ordinary life housed in the People's Palace.

That east end building is a monument to Glasgow's industrial past and those scantly-paid men and women who slaved to make it great and its merchants wealthy.

When I was a teacher in a Maryhill school nearly fifty years ago we'd always the yearly concert in the Burgh Hall. There were big stained-glass windows all round there, showing the different work the Maryhill folk did . . . there was boat-building, blacksmithing, railway work, glass-blowing and other crafts. I think they're maybe in the People's Palace now.

For over ninety years the Palace has been a Mecca for family outings, perhaps they go to reassure themselves that the history of ordinary citizens is no less colourful or important than that of the Tobacco Lords or Merchant Princes.

It wasn't all-that old when I used to go there with my father. We saw all about what the old working-class life had been like and went to the concerts in the Winter Garden . . . and then tea, I remember. He used to say the big glass hall was built like a ship, but I couldn't see that, unless it was upside down.

From over in the west-end of the city come memories that seem to hark back to a more rural past.

I was born in 1900 wi'the century, and reared in Byres Road. My granny used to say th'was cow-sheds there in the old days. Other folk said that was rubbish, that 'Byres' was a man's name. But y'know there was the Cow Loan and the Goose-dubs in the centre of Glasgow; so why no' there on the outskirts? I think I believe my granny.

Some of the recollections of places to the south of the river belong to a pastoral age too . . . like one of Mrs. Nell Dinsmor's.

There was a thatched cottage near us and when I was wee there was a fire there and it was gutted. My father took me in his arms up to see it and watch the fire brigade . . . but so's I wasn't in the way of the sparks.

And there's a picture of craftsmen at work near the village of Pollokshaws.

> There were still weavers in the weavers' cottages beyond the Wellmeadow laundry when I was young . . . old-old cottages they were.

Nearby too, was the aptly-named Picken's orchard.

> . . . opposite the Pollok Park gate. Lovely red apples you got there for a penny.

Unlike other less worthy small boys who knew the place, the speaker virtuously denies ever 'scrumping' them.

> I remember the day old Mr. Picken sold up. I've still got leek-onions in my garden that I got that day, the kind with wee bulbs at the top of the stem. I can still see him standing there telling us to take what we wanted of his raspberry canes or his Egyptian onions, and tears in his eyes.

And no suggestion that the tears were other than those of genuine grief.

The Rodger sisters remember the landmarks and sights of their days in Govan.

> We were brought up there under the big shipyard cran. D'you remember the hooters and the men streaming in and out Stephen's Yard with their piece-boxes? Stephen started with whalers out off the north-east coast somewhere y'know.

Another tale of Govan tells of the origin of the sheep's head carried on the pole in the Govan Fair procession.

> Seems some local minister quarrelled with a young man that was courting the manse maid-servant. Didn't think he was suitable (or maybe he didn't want to lose a good worker) anyway, he wouldn't let the boy come courting. The chap killed one of the minister's best glebe sheep to pay him back. He got the girl in the end and that's why the sheep's head got put on the pole to celebrate.

A happier recollection is cherished of a café at Spiersbridge.

> I minda Capaldi's place opposite the Rouken Glen yonder. It was a big hut sorta place wi' a verandah and fadin' blue paintwork, if I mind

right. And th'was rickety tables where you could sit and lick your slider or poky hat. Or if you were posh, take it from a dish wi' a wee flat wooden spoon. Och aye, and did you ever have a raspberry McCallum?

The city's Tolls and Crosses hold special myths and memories of their own, and the demolition of at least one of those quarters is cursed as desecration. Miss Janet Kay is as outraged about Charing Cross as she was about the destruction in the Ladywell.

Charing Cross! I'll never forgive them for what they did to Charing Cross. Scandalous. It was a landmark. It was *beautiful* . . . And what is it now? Nothing! With a silly half bridge going nowhere.

But then it's maybe a wee while since she's been there to see how 'them' have begun to expiate their sins at Charing Cross. But the same lady knows her Crosses.

Bridgeton Umbrella. D'you know the Bridgeton Umbrella at the Cross? I remember unemployed men . . .

(Sadly so do folk sixty years younger, but those Janet Kay recalls were the workers of the thirties) . . .

. . . standing at the Cross in their bunnets and mufflers. Once when I was very wee I was told that some workmen came along with a ladder, to fix the four-face clock there. The men in the bunnets gave them a hand to sklim up and then went back to the chat or their pitch'n'toss and paid no more heed. Well that night the clock didnae strike, and-here the innards had been stolen. There was just the face left.

The memories move south. John Adamson, knocking out his pipe on what passes for the heart-warming range of his youth, tells of a more ancient legend about a pub near Shawlands Cross, up from Crossmyloof.

Ever since I was wee (and I don't know how long before that) above the doors of that pub at the corner of Langside Avenue there's been a hand with a cross on it. They say that it was at that spot that Mary, Queen of Scots handled her crucifix before the battle of Langside, and swore to fight her enemies 'by the cross on my loof' (hand) . . . It's s'posed to be that that's what gave Crossmyloof its name.

Across the road stood another Shawlands feature of past days.

Th'was a fountain opposite Marlborough House and I mind my mother always telling me no' to drink out the iron cup that used to hang over it on a chain. If you were awful thirsty she said, you'd to hold your finger across between the rim and your lip and drink over that.

A mile south along the road, the Round Toll-house at Pollokshaws is now no more than a clinical, council-used cleaned-up relic of its heyday, isolated on a busy roundabout.

But when I was young it had a lovely rockery in the garden and there was a date-stone lying at the side of the house . . . from the seventeen hundreds sometime. I was upset when that stone disappeared. The lady who lived there when I was small kept hens that scratched about the yard.

Another house recalled from the same early century period is Old Mains House, Giffnock. Miss Jenny and Miss Mabel Logan speak of it.

Old Mains House is mentioned in one of John Galt's books and John Watson who lived there when we were young restored one of the rooms as it would have been in John Galt's time two hundred years ago.

Let's take the route back to town through the old tunnel under the Clyde to another Cross. Miss Christina Ronnie remembers making that journey.

We lived just a stone's throw from the old tunnel with the round buildings at each end . . . where the flowers were a year or two ago (the Garden Festival). We used to walk through to shop at Anderston Cross. Took you out just down from Argyle Street.

There was early car traffic too, from one rotunda to another and Ninette McDonald recalls being part of that.

I went to Park School in town and if I was a bit late I was driven through the tunnel for a short cut.

But, of course it's from the old heart of the city where the pulse

beats faster that the most colourful traditions linger . . . not only
from living memory, but from the days when sheep grazed the
Green, women tubbed their linen and city soldiers drilled there.

> You can still see the place at Glasgow Green where Bonnie Prince
> Charlie reviewed his troops. I'm quite interested in that because my
> own family was divided over the Forty-five, or so they say. And do
> you remember the story about him demanding boots for his army and
> being fobbed off with a whole consignment of boots . . . all for one
> foot.

That's one tale, but someone else was 'no sure about that story'

> There was many a one at that time just had two boots with never a
> difference between right and left anyway . . . so even if it's true maybe
> it wouldnae've mattered.

Long before Bonnie Prince Charlie inspected his army there, or the
Regent Moray raised his standard for the tramp to Langside, the
Green was called the Bishop's forest. It was overgrown, wooded
scrubland for the exclusive use of the cathedral community and its
guests. Over the centuries it has known additions and subtractions
until the days when Janet Kay was taken there as a child . . .

> . . . to see the big Doulton fountain and hear the public speakers ranting
> on about Temperance or Religion or maybe Politics . . . rare speakers
> some of them, mind. Or so my father used to say. I used to get taken
> too, to see what I called 'the iron men'. They're not there now, though
> I'm not sure where they were then. It was just a railing with a man's
> head at the top of each post.*

Not far from where young Janet saw her 'iron men', Peggy
Carson witnessed a sight that must surely have been one of the
last of its kind on the Clyde.

> Would be in the early thirties that I saw a sailing-ship coming in at the
> Broomielaw . . . a sailing ship! My father said it was bringing in paper.
> I've never forgot that ship . . .

*Elspeth King, Glasgow's Depute keeper of local History writes:
    The 'Iron Men' were the main support posts of the cast iron railings between
    Glasgow Green and Monteith Row . . .
and adds that they were stripped out for melting down in the Second War.

And she recalls visits he made with her to the Tent Hall in a street to the east of that brave sight on the river, and things he pointed out to her on the way.

> He used to take me on a Sunday morning to see the free breakfast getting served to the poor and the wee bit entertainment they got along with it. On our road there in the Saltmarket opposite the Briggait, he used to point out the medallion things carved high on the tenements. And–here just recently I saw they were still there . . . all cleaned up with a rose in the middle of one, then a thistle and a daffodil and a shamrock in the others. 'Look up,' my father always used to say, 'Look up, and you'll see things'.

Or 'Look around' he might as easily have said, as another father did in the twenties when he walked across George Square daily to his work.

> He was a great one for giving you wee ways of remembering things . . . like the statues in the Square. It's been seventy years and I can still reel them off.
> 'Poets Campbell, Burns and Scott
> Victoria, Albert, Peel and Watt
> Oswald, Glasgow's first M.P.
> Corunna Moore and Cambell C.
> Gladstone's stony face of flint
> Graham who ran the Royal Mint.'

As a last call for this chapter, it's maybe fitting to make a visit with the late Mr. Tom Watson to the old Tolbooth at the very heart of Glasgow.

> My grandfather told me that because Cameron of Locheil talked Bonnie Prince Charlie out of ransacking Glasgow for not supporting him, the city fathers gave the Camerons the right to have the Tolbooth steeple bells rung for them whenever they visited Glsagow in the future. Still got that right.

But a new age was dawning from that of Tom Watson's grandfather, and there are memories of new toys on Glasgow thoroughfares. Robert Ford remembers . . .

> The first car ever I saw was an Arrol-Johnston '18.

And out in Giffnock Mr. Robert Anderson of Eastwoodhill was
driving another from the same stable, an Arrol-Johnston six-seater.
There was awe at first then, in no time at all, his neighbours were
totting up their savings and following his lead, and soon after an
alarmed local authority felt forced to impose a ten-mile-an-hour
speed limit through the suburb, and the revolution from cartwheels
to Dunlops was underway.

7
Paddys and Biddys

Perhaps life became too earnest when youngsters went to the Big School, too fast moving and with too many different teachers, for the now elderly to be able to pin down as great a number of recollections as they had of younger days. But most of those were vivid and mostly, if not universally, appreciative.

One rememberer recalls doing Latin translation for a redoubtable Classics lady in Hutchesons' Grammar School.

> I got a bit fanciful with the meanings and she just looked at me as she handed back my exercise. 'Isobel Horn, words fail me!'

But they didn't often fail the same sturdy lady with her high bun of hair and trailing gown, and many a Hutchie 'bug' remembers wincing as she boomed out warnings at marching lines winding up the stairs, and yet learning to appreciate her continuing interest in them, long after schooldays. 'Puella stupida!' was a favourite verdict on a struggling pupil.

> That voice, my, my, that voice! She was a one-off . . . unique.

In her turn Janet Kay left Strathclyde Elementary for John Street Higher Grade.

> That was a great school with Mr. Paterson and Miss Fish . . .

and as she passed out with some distinction from their hands, Jimmy Dewar was starting at Shawlands Academy. There's no doubt that, from its first days, Shawlands Academy was a centre of academic excellence, though his account of his homework there does not conjure up a sense of high expectations from teachers or visions of lamp-light slavery to be ready for next day.

> I mostly walked from Pollokshaws Round Toll to Shawlands Cross, but sometimes I took a pennyworth home in the tram. We used to do

our homework on the tram . . . up the stairs and out in the wee front
compartment with the sliding door.

Not a very heavy burden of prep, if it could be accomplished in
the five stops between the Cross and the Round Toll. Perhaps
the sketchy attention to homework was because there was, on
the whole, less awe of teachers in the secondary than in the

elementary school. Older pupils were shrewder too in assessing them as people, and how far they could be pushed. Some, like Mysie Kyle simply sized them up physically.

I remember the headmaster at Whitehill School was called 'Spondy' . . . Spondy Smith . . . because he'd big feet (that was a sort of Latin nickname meaning 'bear's feet').

A door or two along from Spondy's room in the same school reigned Paddy McGlynn remembered by Struan Yule.

All the men teachers were Paddys and the women were Biddys. Anyway we used to do all sorts of things with ink. When we were starting a test maybe one boy would put up his hand and say that he'd no ink. Paddy would say, 'Follow me, boy'. This was to go and get ink. Another boy and then another would join in and there would be a trail of maybe a dozen trudging along after Paddy to get their inkwell filled.

Shrewder teachers brought the ink to the room.

There was this big-big jar of ink wi' the wee spout, kept by the jannie, and if you were top of the class you got taking it round on a Friday to fill the inkwells.

Some waited eagerly for the full well and dropped in a wee lump of calcium carbide to make the ink fizz; others doused bullets of blotting paper and flicked them silently about the room with rulers. And Paddy McGlynn suffered another indignity . . . not with ink though.

He used to report on Schools football for the Evening Times and sat up late writing his column. Sometimes next day he'd nod off and let his bald head drop forward. We used to pick wee crumbs off our rubbers and flick them at his head to waken him up.

The teachers themselves, mind you, weren't above a little backsliding.

I went to Sir John Stirling Maxwell school. I was never any otherwhere in Glasgow for I was away a few years with a sister in Pitlochry after my mother died. I remember two teachers at Sir John's when I was pretty-up in the school. They were in love, I think, and instead of teaching the children they were too busy talking and kissing at the partition door.

Whether such evidence of an amorous liaison would have stood up in court that's how it was seen and rumoured in the playground at the 'Shaws.

But like their elementary counterparts, the Paddys and the Biddys did try to engage their charges in more cultural pursuits, like music and poetry.

We'd one called McIntyre at Whitehill who taught us singing. He told us about projecting the voice and getting the consonants right. A lot paid no attention of course but he was quite easy-osey. 'Please yourselves,' says-he. 'It cost me twenty-five guineas in Milan to learn to do this properly, and here you are getting it for *nothing*'. I quite liked the singing myself though, and I went into the school choir . . . sang 'Who's dat a-calling?' in the City Hall.

As for poetry . . . there were negatives as well as positives to Eileen Reilly's recollections of verse-speaking and its enunciation.

Sometimes we wrote poetry. I wrote one on 'Autumn' and I was very proud of it.

Autumn is a lady who paints the leaves all brown,
She sends them flying in the air to fall upon the groun,

> Singing softly to the roses, she sends them all to sleep,
> She wants us all to love her and mem'ries of her keep.

The priest was in the school that day and I was taken by the teacher to say it aloud to him. They both smiled but I knew fine why, because I wasn't stupid . . . It was because I'd written 'groun' for groun*d*, because that was the way I said it.

Perhaps this carelessness with consonants was repeated at home because we hear next of young Miss Duffy being sent for corrective treatment.

An elocution teacher came to school to take pupils privately, for a small fee. My parents did everything possible for me so I was sent to the elocution. We started by saying familiar words like GIRL. Now here was me thinking I was Glasgow through and through, but I'd been reared by Irish parents and I said Geu'l. The teacher looked shocked at me, 'You can't birl your Rs'. So there was I *branded* as one who couldn't birl her Rs . . . as well as put a D on her groun'! I felt different, inferior. And there was worse, because when I spent the summers in Ireland I was odd man out there too, being *Scottish*. Never mind, I liked the elocution and some of the poems we got to say. But not them all. There was one called 'Mother' . . . kind of sickening really.

> O Mother my love if you give me your hand,
> And go where I ask you to wander,
> I will lead you away to a beautiful land,
> The dreamland that's waiting out yonder . . .
> . . . and I'll rock you asleep on a silver dew stream,
> And sing you to sleep when you're weary,
> And no one shall know of our beautiful dream,
> But you and your own little dearie.

Oh no! that was awful, but I liked one about Kew Gardens.

> Go down to Kew in lilac time,
> In lilac time, in lilac time.
> Go down to Kew in lilac time,
> It isn't far from London.
> And you shall wander hand-in-hand,
> With love in summer's wonderland.
> Go down to Kew in lilac time,
> It isn't far from London.

I liked the rhythms of that.

Schooldays passed eventually and the future beckoned. For most, in early decades, it was the real and earnest world of waged work. For others, more fortunate there were further studies ahead. For a very few it was possible to combine the two. Struan Yule had joined the editorial side of things in *The Glasgow Herald*, on the Stock Market and Business page.

> Since my work then was at night I could go to University classes during the day . . . burned the candle at both ends.

Another student career of those days, not entirely conventional, was that of Miss Jenny Logan.

> It was during the First War so a lot of young men were away and university taboos on women eased a bit. Before that most women who studied at all were at the Normal School (for teacher training) or at Queen Margaret College. So I was in one of the first real mixed classes at university.

At that time and for thirty more years the University of Strathclyde was still the 'Tech'.

> When I went there first we heard a lot about the founder John Anderson. They called him Jolly Jack Phosphorus . . . some said because he was a chemist, others that he'd a fiery temper.

Not everyone enjoyed further education.

> I went to university, Gilmorehill, but I didn't like it much. I did get a First Class Honours degree in Modern Languages . . . but a bonnie lot of good it did me. I taught for a time in a small private school for girls . . . not very well known. It didn't survive.

Nor, as a reluctant teacher, did that rememberer. Perhaps her first choice would have been music but that didn't seem to the family 'safe' and she was denied it.

> I think I was allergic to education . . . unless it was something I really wanted to do.

At either of those degree-course establishments the young spent three or more years . . . long enough to enjoy the traditional college life-style. Others equally qualified, but for whom the need was more pressing to put in their pennyworth to the household kitty, took shorter courses or went to evening classes.

I went to night school in the twenties to learn book-keeping. You got
your first year free. But I kept on going until I was twenty-one.

I'd to take a job whenever I left school. But I'd an uncle helped me to
go to classes and I learned a lot there about business. Later I was able to
set up as a kind of agent for ironmongery an' that. Did very well really
but that was thanks to my uncle. And he wasn't all that well-off.

It's a hundred and twenty years since Glasgow School Boards
had all its youngsters compulsorily with a Paddy or Biddy. In the
1960s, and retired after a long career of teaching in city schools,
Jenny Logan continued to put the experience of those years to
use delving into the educational archives in the basement of the
City Chambers. This was in preparation for celebrations at the
centenary of official schooling. Maybe she discovered that here,
and there and elsewhere in Scotland, a child slipped through the
net and did not enjoy his or her full entitlement of sand trays and
subtraction, books and beltings. Take young Alex Donnelly born
in Calton thirty years after that Education Act.

My father was killed at the Dardenelles when I was thirteen. There
were five younger than me so I just had to leave the school.

But if that seems like the end of education for Master Donnelly,
tune in to other chapters and follow his appetite for self-
improvement.

Another of the same breed was Mr. Robert Ford, who started
life in Portpatrick.

I'd three miles to walk to the school. I was wee for my age so I didnae
go till I was seven. They weren't so partic'lar in those days. Then
the Great War came and with me being twelve and about two years
behind, and my father having the croft, I just left the school to work
with him. Anybody that could work the land was just let work. So I'd
just the five years at school.

Like Alex Donnelly he refused to leave it at that.

Later on I went to night-school and was taken on by a joiner. I learned
that trade and studied geometry and other subjects till I was over thirty.
But I'd always missed out on English so I took an interest myself in
poetry, wrote some and read some and learned quite a lot by heart

> . . . Cocker and Service and Scott and, of course Burns . . . going to
> Burns' Suppers with James Currie and so on, y'know . . .

Robert Ford had done it the hard way but as he sits now going
over some of his own verses, reminiscing in the suburban home
built fair and square with his own skilled hands . . . and declaring
without a note over a hundred lines of William Landles' narrative
poem 'Herod and John' it can only be said that Portpatrick's loss
was Glasgow's gain and that his self-acquired education has served
him as well as most who had twice as long at school.

8

Nellie Kelly Smoked a Pipe

They talk a lot these days about modern work expertise and the sophisticated high-tech education required to master it. But looking across the whole range of waged occupations of eighty and ninety years ago, remembered here, one gets the feeling that the young of the 1990s might easily find the skills of their 'simple' forebears quite beyond them.

Before describing their own life-work many rememberers recalled that of parents and grandparents, often hard darg unbuffered by Health Insurance . . . no work, no money.

Perhaps the earliest livelihood spoken of, was that earned by Mrs. Agnes Grove's great-grandfather who kept a pub in the Cubie Street area about the time that George IV and William IV were on the throne in the 1820s and 1830s. But it's the work of her own father that she recalls as an everyday part of her own early life.

> He was a tailor and cutter. He'd been at the Buchanan Institute near the Glasgow Green when he was young. It was for fatherless boys and they were taught trades there. It was the tailoring for him. His mother would be working, so he had all his meals there too. I remember him working at home . . . in the Room . . . legs crossed on the table. Said that's how he was bow-legged. But all tailors sewed like that, to keep their materials up beside them. When he was making a suit I had to pick up all the clippings . . . that was called 'the woollen' and my mother sold it at the rag store for a few pence.

Her grandmother was in textiles too, working a Jacquard loom in Templeton's.

Aye, the Doges' Palace* y'know. And she used to take me up by
Parkhead and Tollcross, and through the windows you could see in
the single-ends some of the handloom weavers doing piecework with
home looms . . . eighty years ago, easy.

That was weaving on quite a heavy-weight scale, but Mrs.
Millicent Davis's grandfather worked with finer materials.

He was a silk merchant trading a lot in the Far East. There was a
man he dealt with in Prestwick (it was quite a remote village in my
grandparents' time). He was called Rab and he was one of the last of
a colony of handloom silk weavers. Rab was very old at the end of last
century so he must have been working in early Victorian times. I still
have some of his silk . . .

*The architects of Templeton's carpet factory, built in 1889 to replace the original
mill, designed it as a replica of the Doges' Palace in Venice.

. . . a hundred years old now, a prized possession reverently handled and shown off.

Dr. Ellis Barnett cherishes memories of his father Bernard, another of those young Jewish men of the early century whose sufferings in Lithuania drove him to 'get on a boat' to look for better things elsewhere. After some years learning his trade in South Africa, 'elsewhere' became the Glasgow Gorbals where he set up as a shoemaker in Crown Street and quickly endeared himself to the community.

> It was a tough place then with youngsters roaming wild and breaking windows. Instead of chasing them my father started what he called the 'Gorbals Pals Club' with about four hundred in it. He had membership cards for them and gave every one a Saturday penny every week . . . ticked their cards to stop them coming twice.

The shop was a kind of Lost Property depot too.

> If a child got lost in the Gorbals he always knew how to get to my father's shop and his mother would find him there.

Small wonder his clientele, when they were solvent, bought their shoes from him.

> He'd once a man just out of jail coming in for shoes when he hadn't even a pair of socks on his feet. He bought the shoes and got the socks free.

Even when he prospered, Bernard's tastes remained simple.

> He'd a small office and when a wealthy acquaintance asked why he didn't get himself a big place like the man's own, he had a typical reply. 'Friend,' he said. 'One day you and I will both be in a smaller place than this. It'll be a shock for you. But not for me.'

Another, feeling his way in a new culture was Mrs. Lily Joseph's father from Russia. He found work close to where the immigrant community had settled.

> Came here in 1897 and got his first job where a lot of foreigners worked, at a tobacco factory near the Saltmarket Bridge.

Perhaps one of his workmates was Lily Balarsky's mother, a lady

with drive and the adaptability to leave lack of opportunity behind
and turn her hand to anything in her adopted country.

> They were ready to try whatever turned up and when she first came
> to Glasgow she worked, like a lot of Jewish folk, rolling cigarettes at
> a factory not far from where they lived.

Her father was flexible too and had several strings to his bow.

> He was a jack-of-two-or-three trades. He mainly sold drapery from a
> suitcase . . . all over Scotland. Then he'd a wee sideline with a friend
> in Oxford Street who was very good at repairing watches my father
> collected on his rounds. And another line was selling lengths of tartan
> cloth that a friend wove. I went with him to Invergordon to sell bits
> and pieces and the tartan to English sailors. We went out to a navy ship
> in a wee ferry. And at home I used to run to Oxford Street to deliver
> and collect the watches.

Millicent Davis's other grandfather worked on a grander engineering scale than watchmaking.

> He built the big crane at Govan. It was a landmark, the biggest in the
> world at one time.

And perhaps even grander than that, must have been the proud
task of Mr. Rodger, the skilled operator who worked it.

> My father driv the big Govan crane . . . for years. Then one day he
> took a shock up there on it and he never worked again. I was just
> young then.

What Ann Hutchison's father driv was his beloved horse,
Nancy, and his pride was in the quality of his firewood.

> He'd a real nice cart with his logs and briquettes and sticks. It was never
> rubbish wood my Daddy sold . . . never yon dry rot stuff . . . not at
> all! He used to take his cart to Port Glasgow and bring back pine logs.
> Oh, what a lovely smell! We'd all to help chop it into wedges then bag
> it to sell for about a shilling a bag.

There are niceties in every job and Mr. Hutchison observed his
own tight code of behaviour.

> He never-ever shouted from his cart, my Daddy, not like some.
> Never. He'd his regulars every week that he went round just.

Two who would have approved of his fine wood were Struan Yule's father and grandfather.

> Everything to do with wood my grandfather did. Early on he was a brewers' cooper, then a joiner, cabinet-maker and funeral undertaker. My father was a cabinet-maker too.

Alex Donnelly's recollections of his father's trade give a real glimpse into a couthy old Scottish world, long long gone and scarcely remembered now. He too was a skilled craftsman . . . his medium not wood but clay.

> Aye, my father had a wee clay-pipe work in the Gallowgate. I used to play guns wi' the moulds there. They'd to serve seven year to be a right pipe-maker. They got the clay fae Cornwall, steeped the big block in a byne of water to soften it. Then they cut off a slobbery dod and divided it up into bits like a bunch of bananas. They pushed each one into a half mould wi' the name DONNELLY engraved on it and got a needle thing to make the bore in the stem. The women trimmed the mould and put the extra back into the clay. No waste see. Then they touched it up all neat and put the two sides together and polished it. Each worker had her own number on wee cubes of clay and she put them beside her finished pipe . . . piece-work see. Men got the pipes free in the pubs wi' their pints. Other places it was a ha' penny or a penny. Forbye the pipes, they made pipe-clay squares for doin' the closes . . . farthing a square . . . In Ireland later, when I was busking, you often seen a couple there havin' puff about of the one clay, by their turf fire. No' many women in Glasgow smoked the pipe but. No' when I was young.

An eavesdropper knew one though . . .

> . . . old Nellie Kelly that worked for us did.

Real Glasgow that, clay-pipes and pipe-clay. So too were the toffee 'balls' and the 'ginger' made at the factory run by Mysie Kyle's father and destined for sale at the city's oldest building.

> When my father had the lemonade and toffee-making place he supplied Mistress Haddow in the wee shop in Provand's Lordship. The bottles went in wooden crates on the horse-lorry. For making the toffee he'd a hook on the wall and he took the hot toffee with flour on his hand and pulled and stretched it till it was golden, then he mixed it with the

dark stuff, rolled it out so it was striped, and then cut it up.

Poles apart from that old Glasgow, and seemingly bizarre in the midst of city life, except perhaps as a lingering echo of a more rural town of 17th century cottages and grazings, is the home Christina Ronnie and her sister Mary Brisbane remember from their youth. Mrs. Ronnie first . . .

> I was born in a two-room and kitchen tenement in McLean Street, Plantation, out Govan Road. My mother was a farmer there with cows and chickens and there were horses in the stable there. Th'was a big backcourt for all the houses and the cows were in a cobbled pend. She used to take them up Craigwell Street Wee-Brae to the grazing in a field over Ibrox way. I never heard of any other farm like that. The byre was in the back too and th'was a dung midden. My mother worked hard, milking the cows and that, and in the dairy she had, on the front street. I still have her milking-stool and the wee tub she had for making butter. And I always mind when she worked wi' the cows she wore what was called a 'shorgun'. It came to just below the waist and th'was wide petticoats under that, and a sacking apron. My father was an invalid so we depended on her wi' the farm and the dairy. She sold her own butter and eggs and milk there . . . and baking. She needed us too. 'Chrissie,' she'd say before school in the morning, 'churnin' the night, mind. Hurry home.' The churning with the first plunger-churn we had was like doin' washing the old way . . . plunge and twist, plunge and twist. Then we got a barrel one, with a handle to caw. All I got for doing that was a drink of buttermilk wi' the wee pearls of butter left in it. No pay. It was hard.

A man who by then was devoting his working energies to making life more than bare survival for such families was a neighbour of Mrs. Dinsmor's family in Barrhead.

> My father was friendly with Jimmy Maxton, and my mother with his sister, Annie. (Jimmy was a widower and Annie brought up young Jimmy that I played with.) Many's the time I was in that house. He was a gentle, nice man Jimmy Maxton and he worked hard. There's a Maxton garden now in Barrhead that was put there by his friends in the House of Commons, even in other parties. Churchill put to it too. He was that popular. The M.P. for Bridgeton he was, I.L.P.

But friendship can be stretched too far for a strict mother to thole.

For a while my father took us to the I.L.P. Sunday school. Not for long though. My mother was a Quaker and saw to it that we went to the right Sunday School.

Apart from Millicent Davis's family, who had a three-generation connection with Fairfield's, there wasn't much dynastic continuity in the work of most rememberers. A few skills descended to a son or daughter but, as technical progress made their crafts redundant, seldom further. Of those few the young Rodgers of McLean Street had little alternative at first to carrying on at least part of their mother's work. Mary, now Mrs. Brisbane, remembers her share in that.

After my mother died we gave up the cows, but we kept on the chickens and the dairy. We bought in butter and milk for that. Folk used to come in for one egg, a pennyworth of milk, a wee loaf and a penny packet of tea. Dockers just got twelve shillings a week then . . . before 1920. My oldest sister did the shop but I used to go out at six o'clock in the morning before school wi' the milk in cans, a whole row of them clattering on my arm . . . two-pint, one-pint and half-a-pint. I'd to chap all the doors up the closes, up four stairs, then collect the emptied cans on the way down again. Cream too . . . just a gill people would get.

All the Rodger brothers went off to sea.

They went as 'dunkey' men, that was ships' greasers. So th'was just the girls left at home. It was hard times. Nothing coming in but from the dairy. The area got to be rundown and rough-spoken. But we never-ever swore or anything. My mother wouldn't't've had that at all. I was behind yon counter from ten-year-old and full-time at fourteen. We'd the big ten-gallon cans to scour and scald, and when the boats came in up the Clyde at night we'd to open up and sell them bread and milk and that. Later the factor gave us a better shop across the road.

When their mother died Chrissie took over the house and the nursing of their father.

May was young at the school at first, and my other sister Effie done the shop. (Mind I had delivered the early morning milk for a while . . . got exemption from the school till half-past nine for that) but I was fourteen now and I was to be in charge of the house, and nursing my father for the next five years till he died. I'd to bath him every Sunday.

Income was low and state help non-existent, and when the girls were finally left alone it was big decision time for Chrissie.

I couldnae think to stay in the house and I wasnae one for the shop so I decided that it would be a help if I went into service. Effie and May didnae like it, but I went temporary to my first place, that was to a part of the family that Angus Ogilvie's of now. I went to Gryffe Castle, Bridge of Weir . . . done the kitchen work and the cooking there. Then I went back to the Domestic Registry for another place. A lady looking for someone interviewed me there for a scullery maid rising to cooking. Her place was at Comlongen Castle near Dumfries. I said 'Aye' I would dae't. She pushed a shilling across the table. 'What's that for?' says-I. She said it was my word that I would come, and her word that she would have me.

So Christina Rodger was 'arled' to Comlongen Castle and into a long life of Service. We can't follow her here through the list of her fortunes and misfortunes, colleagues, employers and kitchens: the skinning of game, the plucking of fowl, the burnishing of copper, the high life of the London Season in Park Lane, the romance begun when she was in 'Dunragit Big Hoose'. There's a novel in there somewhere, but not for these pages and we must leave her, earning her monthly two pounds and sending home the precious share of it to make things easier in McLean Street.

The old building there . . . everything's away now, nothing left.

Except the recipe for the dairy's dumpling, of which a delectable slice was carried home by the compiler of these notes after her meeting with Mrs. Brisbane.

Agnes Grove was another who followed family footsteps, though not at first.

I went to the paper-bag-making near Glassford Street when I left school. You done all the folding and pasting and you got fivepence for a thousand bags. You'd to get quick at it or starve! But then I

went into Templeton's . . . not the big building at first, but the shed
at the back. Ocht, but Templeton's was better'n the paper pokes. It
was treadle looms and we wove the chenille to be wound round big
drums to go and be made into carpets.

'Chenille' was for the French 'caterpillar' and described the hairy
surface produced by the loom on one side of the fabric which,
bonded to a jute backing, James Templeton had long before
realised would make a sturdy carpet.

At the looms you worked from a chart card that told you how
many shots to do in this or that colour, twelve shuttle shots to
the inch. I always wanted to see the finished article, but you never
did. The backing was done at a factory in West Street. You got five
shillings a week for the fortnight you learned, and when you got
your own loom you'd to pay back that ten shillings before you got
any more pay. That was all early in the century. Templeton's did the
carpet for the White House Oval Room y'know, and for the *Queen
Mary*.

After a variety of schoolboy jobs Jimmy Dewar went to sea. His
father had been a sea-travelling salesman, but Jimmy was a bona
fide sailor.

Magical life it was. Before that I was in a stevedore's office, but all I
could think of were the wonderful ships coming in from Hong Kong,
Malaya, Yokohama. So I joined a ship and started off to sea . . . all
over the world, into all the ports. I loved it.

While this son of Glasgow was off on his travels the Servadei
family arrived.

It was mostly ice-cream, that Italians went into . . . don't know why
really. Very few of them made it in Italy. But it was an opening here.
That and fish and chips. Don't get them in Italy either. Hairdressing
was another thing. My father had trained as a hairdresser in Genoa
and when he came here before the First War he worked at that for an
uncle. Then he set up on his own and when I grew up I went in with
him.

Angelo Lamarra settled for the ice-cream . . . at first in the way
most familiar of all to four generations of young Scotland.

I went out at first pushing an ice-cream barrow in Falkirk . . . STOP

ME AND BUY ONE y'know . . . all round the streets. Then we came to Glasgow and I worked in a café in Parliamentary Road, purely a café . . . the real thing y'know, marble tables with iron legs. I served over the counter too.

Then he graduated to that other matchless skill of the true Glasgow Italian.

. . . a fish 'n chip shop at 794 Garscube Road. My brother and I tried our own shop for a while, but that was a flop and we went to work for the Castelvecchis in Paisley . . . the thirties . . . an awful bad time for drunks coming in to pick fights, much worse than later. Then the war came and I was interned. But I was engaged to be married by then and my young lady worked awful hard . . . took on a café and had it paid off by the time I came back. Then we'd another place, rough with street fights outside . . . maybe I'm easy scared but I didn't like that. Then when this place here, 'The Trees', came on the market we took a big breath and bought it. No trouble here, never-ever, and we're busy. D'you know I'm so happy here I wish I could live to be a million.

Like Mrs. Grove, Bunty Angles had a go at something else before settling to her real career.

I was in a sweetie shop, but I only lasted a week because the woman kept asking if I was eating the sweeties or touching the money. My grandmother wasn't going to have that, so I left. After that it was fashion shops. Wallace's in Maryhill first, learning to serve and to poke the money into yon wee cups, twist them and scoosh them up to the cashier. I was in Dresses at Wallace's. Then I went to Colthart's in Queen Street. I became a buyer there . . . used to go to London to see the Collections and choose what would sell in Glasgow. I'd always to be well-dressed, and that was nice . . . no overalls or anything.

Lily Balarsky was at the creative end of the same business, inheriting her skills and economies from her mother, who'd had to build and furbish home and family from nothing bar the candlesticks from Lithuania.

She never wasted a scrap of material, made all sorts of things with her cuttings. Sewed all our clothes so we'd always nice things to wear. I became a dressmaker too, I was apprenticed to the Barbacks' establishment at Eglinton Toll . . . three sisters had it. Miriam became very well known. They did beautiful work . . . very strict taskmasters, but good teachers. It was first class training. From there I went as an alteration hand to the Morrisons' Group, and I did dress-making from home.

In her young days Mrs. Mysie Kyle's was the skilled hand that added the finishing touches . . . the crown of glory to an Angles' London gown or a Balarsky original.

I learned to be a milliner at Daly's when I left school. Very posh. I got seven shillings a week there. That would be the twenties. Sometimes it was re-blocking and trimming customers' hats, sometimes making them up new. We all sat round four big tables to work and, later, when I was 'head of the table' I got thirty shillings or two pounds. Sometimes you were sent downstairs to serve. That was a wee change, but lots of ladies came in just to try on hats and the manager didn't like you not getting sales. I gave up that work when I got married. You had to. Didn't keep married women on.

Earlier than that, Lily Joseph was in 'eggs'.

When I left school my third sister's husband was in the egg business. I had been to college to learn the shorthand and typing, but when he opened his place in Adelphi Street we all went into the eggs. My mother too. And we sold a home-made drink too that was awful good. He was a marvel my third sister's husband. He was well-off but he shared . . . good to us all.

Ann Hutchison was thirled to the house.

. . . but my sisters had jobs in Pollokshaws, one at the weavin' and one at the pottery. I think it was in Cogan Street. You used to could see the wet clay runnin' out at the back . . . awful messy. Th'were a funny thing though. Some of the pottery pieces had MADE IN IRELAND on the bottom. Maybe they sold better for bein' a bit kinda foreign.

Perhaps in another context the Shanks' Patents referred to by Nell Dinsmor could be loosely, and doubly, called 'pottery' too.

Barrhead was always famous for that. I knew a man in the Company and when he went on holiday he was more interested in the cludgies than the fancy places or the sight-seeing.

Robert Ford, having left school after only his five years there, to work on his father's seven-acre croft at Portpatrick, nevertheless struck out independently into his own line of work, his own further education and finally into successful business for himself.

After my father's place I was waged on to a farm and got about fifteen pounds at the end of six months. This was at the end of the First War. You worked wi' your bare feet all the time except maybe for the very hard winter. Your feet got tough like that . . . leathery. Saved your boots. Anyway, fifteen pounds for six months of working, five in the morning to eight at night. The cows were to milk night and morning. D'you know it was 1931 before ever I saw a milk bottle? My parents lived very sparse and whatever else was spent, fifty pounds was always kept for funerals.

Small wonder he lost the notion for farming and went to learn the joinery.

It was mostly horse-carriages and wheels I started on, but by the time my four years was up nob'dy wanted horse-carriages. So I went to night school to learn about building and do maths.

'Nob'dy' might want horse-carriages but tramcars were in their prime.

I came to Glasgow for work and went to Coplaw Street tram depot.

That was 1929, and I was working closing up the open-end trams
. . . glassing them in. Took eighteen months to do them all, then
we were paid off. It was bad times, 1930, to get a job, so I started
up my own wee business in Kinning Park . . . rented the old byre the
Rodgers sisters had given up. After that I was in Plantation there for
thirty-eight years. Wheelbarrows was my main line at first . . . my
speciality. There was hods for builders, and bakers' trays too, for
Peacock's and Ross's Dairies and Price Brothers. Then th'was the wee
war ladders as well.

And three entire houses built with his own skeely hands and the
mathematics knack he had learned at the night-school long ago.
The vandalism of the sixties, and unsympathetic officialdom,
finally drove him to retirement, to the books and poetry he had
come to with such pleasure, long after his brief schooldays.

It wasn't only Robert Ford's glassed-in tramcars that took
people to their work, there were the trains remembered by Jack
Roche.

Most folk out Calton way worked in the tobacco or one of the mills
there, but a lot of Bridgeton people had jobs at Clydebank . . . Singer's
or John Brown's. I worked for a while as a guard on the trains going
that way. Th'was what was cried the 'First Brig'ton' and the 'Second
Brig'ton' . . . one early in the morning and one later.

Perhaps those who worked so far from home had fewer perks than
the locals who could walk home from work in Clydebank.

Th'was a thing they used to say . . . that Clydebank did a roaring trade
in the fallin's off of the yard lorries. Aye, that nearly the whole of
Clydebank was furnish'd, court'sy John Brown . . . first class fittin's
and furniture . . . carpets even.

Those living too far to make such 'economies' possible, *and* the
virtuous, were indignant.

. . . mind a lot were real cocky about their pilfers, blowed about them
. . . right gallus.

Not all recollected skills were manual. Miss Isobel Horn and
Struan Yule were wordsmiths in their working life.

I was desperate to get into journalism, but the nearest I could get at first

was writing advertising copy for Copland and Lye. Then I got a chance
to go on the Women's Rural Institute Magazine. That was great . . .
did some of the editorials and went out interviewing and reporting on
branch meetings. Did that for seven years, then had to do war work.
Eventually I got back and became the editor. I travelled a lot then to all
the country places. I visited the Castle of Mey once. The Institute had
sewn a boudoir set for the Queen Mother . . . a couch coverlet and a
cushion and a hot bottle cover. Then she invited the Caithness branch
to the castle to see them in place.

More mundanely there was the matter of the cleekit gloves . . .
just as knacky but more down-to-earth.

We answered queries too and I remember one about these 'cleekit'
gloves. Have you ever heard of cleekit work? It was quite a *man*'s
craft.

And here the long arm (or deft hand) of coincidence brings the
quirk of the same incident being related quite separately by two
people now living sixty miles apart. The cleekit gloves query had
been from Millicent Davis.

I once saw a pair of these gloves in a craft shop. They were a dreadful
colour and I didn't buy them. But I was always sorry after. I knew
cleekit work when I saw it, but I didn't know how it was done. I wrote
to The Scottish Field and got a few replies. 'My father (or grandfather
or the grieve) made them', sort of answer. But they didn't know how.
Later I got a little piece done by a lady in Canada and I tried it myself
with an old hook like a thorn, but not properly. Then someone said I
should write to Miss Horn of the W.R.I. magazine. She put my letter
into the next issue and I got a lot of information from all over.

And Isobel Horn . . .

Later we gave a copy of the directions free to anyone who would make
gloves for our Conference sales table. Oh, it was an interesting life on
the magazine.

Many another Dennistoun man was a 'killer' in the meat market,
earning big money, but from school there, Struan Yule set his
sights on *The Glasgow Herald* . . . preferably the Editor's chair
and as soon as possible.

I applied by letter and there was a wee delay in getting a reply, so I thought my letter had got lost in the post and I went to see them. Said I was interested in a job on the editorial side.

'Oh!' says the man, 'everyone starts here on the post desk.'

'Well,' says I, 'as long as it's not for too long.'

In spite of his nerve he was appointed and after his obligatory stint with the letters, spent the whole of his working life there in the Business Section.

We'll look elsewhere at another side of Alex Donnelly's career on Glasgow's entertainment scene in his fiddling days, but he earned a more prosaic bawbee in a variety of other lines.

When my father got killed in the First War the clay-pipe factory got sold off and I left the school at thirteen and went to the Co-op as a message-boy at five shillings a week . . . carried the basket on my head on a wee round cushion like a black puddin'. After that I worked in The Castle pub in Calton, then in Rowan's boiler shop, screwin' rods for big-big forty-ton ships' boilers.

All the while, of course, practising the music, against hard times.

I used to knock the gas mantles off wi' my bow, so when I met this fella that was sellin' an old tin saxophone I bought it and learned that . . . and then a mandolin. I earned a bit extra that way. You just did ever'thing you could. Eventually me and my wife took a newsagent's shop in Oatlands and another in Eglinton Street. Ocht aye, you'd to turn your hand to anything.

Not many could turn theirs to such a plethora of skills though.

And that 'turning the hand to anything' says it for all of them really . . . the cooks, the dressmakers, the restaurateurs and the milliners, the joiners, the pipe-makers and the scribes. None made fortunes. None claimed brilliance. But all unconsciously radiated a sort of sensible Glasgow pride in their own crafts well done.

9

Tea and a Hot Co-op Pie

Family outings in Edwardian times, sometimes by the whole tribe, sometimes by only assorted members, came in a variety of forms, depending on weather, pocket, season or what parents thought was for the ultimate health and welfare of their offspring.

The most sedate came under the heading of Visiting, a much less casual activity than the mug-in-the-hand or barbecue of the 1990s. There would be the prim walk to the host house, the handing over of the small present or the bunch of flowers. Then, once embraced by Auntie and patted on the head by Uncle, the Visit was in progress. The visit could be 'from' as well as 'to', but the niceties, although reversed, were the same. Miss Ann Hutchison remembers both coming and going for high tea.

> Oh, we went visiting right-enough, We'd an Aunt McKenzie in Tassie Street that we went to reg'lar. And we *had* visitors. We'd my Daddy's brother and his wife every second Sunday for their tea.

There would be 'knife and fork'.

> And there would be baking on the range for that visit.

After the meal of cold ham or fish or ham-and-eggs, plain bread and butter, tea-bread and cake, there often came the formal entertainment. Jean Paterson was one performer.

> You'd always to do your 'turn'. Stand up in front of everyone in the room and say a poem or maybe do your newest piece on the piano . . . your Farmyard Tunes or Joys for Ever.

Week-end visiting was a multicultural activity. Certainly the immigrant communities used it to keep in touch with their own roots. Mario Servadei recalls . . .

Our family life was very Italian I suppose. You integrated right-enough during the week, but Saturday and Sunday you kept close to relatives on a visiting basis. It was just visiting. They're still done, Italian things, but not so much now. Some have even given up the 'i' at the end of their names . . . maybe a Rossi becoming Ross. And yet even after a generation or so, a bit of you still feels Italian. Maybe that visiting helped you to feel part of Italy.

And Mrs. Lily Joseph looks back to immigrant days in her circle.

> The Jewish community kept close for support and because of language and religion and all the customs. We did a lot of visiting, informal get-togethers, sometimes in houses but other times in the synagogue. We'd sing songs, tell real stories about the Jewish past . . . say poems maybe.

Perhaps a foretaste of the casual culture that was coming can be detected in a memory of Nell Dinsmor's. Or maybe it looked casual because it concerned the breaking-out of one of a protected and confined species, the dutiful daughter-at-home.

> I had this aunt, the unmarried one at home. She would be s'posed to be shopping in Shawlands, but here instead she'd take the blue Renfrew Ferry tram to her sister's in Barrhead to get tea and a hot Co-op pie. She wouldn't tell at home but she'd kind of rebelled a wee bit.

Then for most youngsters there were parties, both given and gone to. There they ate their buns and their Playmate biscuits over a crumb sheet sensibly tacked to the floor over a prized carpet and they learned the repertoire of singing games for socially correct tots. These were the activities that came before the sophisticated kissing games that were heady stuff for teenagers.

> Och, you didnae call them 'teenagers' then. Anyway early-on you played 'Here we go gathering nuts in May', 'The Farmer's in the Dell' 'Musical Chairs', 'Water Water Wallflower' or 'Broken Bridges'. Later it was 'Postman's Knock', 'Winkie', 'Cushiony' and 'The Grand Old Duke of York' . . . you did kissing at them.

There were times when parties were illicit excursions, even if entirely innocent once in progress. Mrs. Jean Walker has a tale of her mother as a determined gate-crasher . . . not *into* the party but out of her own home to get to it.

> My grandmother was dead so my mother was brought up by a housekeeper around the Gorbals somewhere. One time she was invited to a Jewish girl's party and the housekeeper said 'no' she couldn't go. But this Jewish girl was her friend, so she just turned her pinafore to the clean side and went.

There were other parent-figures too who didn't always give their blessing to parties . . . not birthday parties anyway. Mrs. Agnes Grove's father was suspicious of *motive* and said so bluntly to a mother who lived to rue the fact that she hadn't heard of crumb drugget.

> My father didn't believe in birthday parties. 'Present parties' he called them. If you're to give a party, give a party just. So maybe at Hallowe'en my mother'd make champit tatties with trinkets in. But not after once when the tatties got tramped into the carpet. After that it was dumplings and sing-songs and dookin' for apples . . . or treacle scones hanging from the pulley that you'd to catch in your mouth, with your hands behind your back. That was messy too mind, but only on your face.

It was a very rare house in which there was an easy, hand-in-pocket supply of money; and bought treats were seldom enough to be real occasions. For the Hutchison brood the briquette-and-sticks business yielded an annual season of two outings.

> Every year my Daddy treated us to two things, the pantomime and the Kelvin Hall carnival. That cost a bit too much money, but he always did it, and we got our teas as well.

Alongside the carnival was the circus, favoured by some over the push-penny and the roundabouts.

> I liked the circus righ'enough an' Dave Willis at the pantomime (sic). He was awful good. D'you mind his wee Injun song?
> All dress'd up in m'Injun fea-thers
> Listen to the talkin' Injun ble-thers
> Me an' my squaw an' my wee papoose
> My wigwam's better'n a cooncil hoose.

Two outings seemed to be the done thing in the Festive Season.

> We always used to go to two pantomimes . . . Tommy Lorne at The Royal, and George West at The Princess's. There was always thirteen letters in the name of The Princess's pantomime. They weren't your traditional Cinderella or Mother Goose or that. There was the likes of 'Tammytoorytap' then later, after I was grown up th'was 'The Tintock Cup'. One year my father must've taken a notion to one

of the Principal Boys and got me to write for a signed photo. It didn't go on *my* wall with my film stars. It disappeared into *his* desk.

That was the panto scene with the gorgeous Harry Gordon, the lancer-prancing Dave Willis of the cherry nose and wee moustache, Tommy Lorne with his lugubrious gawkiness, and all the rest with their 'feeds' and leggy Principal Boys.

But the spectacle that took the breath away more than any of those was surely Hengler's circus, for it is recalled by almost every rememberer who had a Glasgow childhood in its heyday. Mrs. Mysie Kyle has nothing to say of pantomimes or carnivals . . .

No, we didn't get taken to pictures or theatres but we did to go to Hengler's Circus . . . oh my, Hengler's circus!

There was more to this performance than traditional circus acts. Music-hall type turns were inserted here and there throughout the programme.

I mind of someone singing 'On Mother Kelly's Doorstep' and doing some kind of parody on that. And th'was other song and dancing acts. I mind too, at the hall where Hengler's was held, that at other times you got to watch lantern slides for a penny on Saturday afternoons.

Mrs. Bunty Angles went to the circus performances when they took place near St. George's Cross.

There was always Doodles the Clown at Hengler's. He was good was Doodles . . . clever clown. Everybody loved Doodles.

For some the animals were the real stuff of the circus.

It was the lions and the lion-tamer that I remember. I was taken every year by an uncle, with my wee sister. There was a cage dropped round the arena with the lions and this lion-tamer in it, in his riding breeches and white polo neck. He'd a long-handled whip that he cracked, and the first time he did it one year, my wee sister thought he was whipping the lions and she screamed so much I'd to take her outside till the next act came on.

The horses were good. There was a thing about one being able to distinguish colours by name. The man used to say 'I'm putting the

blue cloth at this side . . .' and 'I'm putting the red cloth at the other
side'. Then he would get the horse to bring him the one he asked for.
He would try and cheat the horse and change them over, but the horse
never got confused. I thought it was magic.

But lions, clowns, magic . . . whatever else, the most vivid,
marvellous memory of all is of the climax to the performance.
Bunty Angles has it spotlit and sharp from her pre-First War
childhood.

It was the Indian shooting the rapids scene. There would be a beam of
light picking out the Chief Brave that stood away up high above the
arena. The floor went down then the water rushed into some kind of
circular tank and the Indians and horses were in and across it yowling
and doing their war cries.

Miss Isobel Horn speaks for a whole generation.

The water scene at the end . . . great stuff! Dramatic and wild!

And there's an intangible something that always brings Hengler's
rushing back to Struan Yule.

When I smell oranges, the circus always comes to mind. People
ate oranges at shows because they made less noise than sweetie
papers.

That then, was Hengler's circus; but the aroma of oranges, and
the sweetie papers they replaced, also hung about the venue of
another well-loved social and moral institution that was part of
the fabric of life in former days. While the Band of Hope may
not have been founded principally for entertainment its young
adherents certainly look back on the malarky rather than the
precepts of the Friday night out. Struan Yule was no better than
the rest.

We always bought toffees on Band of Hope night. The toffees were good
but as well as that you could stick the papers on each other's noses.
    At the swarry you got a bag of buns and an orange. Th'was always
oranges at the Band of Hope. I always think on the two together, the
oranges and the Band of Hope.

And the wicked Struan Yule again . . .

The Reverend James Muir B.D. was the boss of our Band of Hope. When we'd lantern slides that moved along in strips of four pictures (Y'know the sort of thing . . . poor wee waif with the drunken father) well, the minister sat down at the front and clicked his fingers for the change of picture. In no time at all everyone cottoned on and we'd all be clicking away to hurry them on and get to the tea or the oranges.

All the same they signed the pledges and learned the slogans that have stuck in the mind for seventy and eighty years. 'Strong drink is a mocker' 'Think . . . not drink!' and they can still chant even their own wee rhymes that parodied yet echoed official policy.

> Look on spirits as your foe
> Make your answer ever 'No'!
> See the drunkards o'er the edge
> Keep yer heid and sign the pledge.

When the winter was past and the time for the singing of birds was come, it was the great outdoors that beckoned, and families put panto and circus into moth balls until next December and took to the highways and byways for their outings. Mary Brisbane was a sprig of a robust family of walkers.

> People just did walk in those days . . . that was before the First War. I'd an uncle used to walk from Glasgow to Greenock and back. Reg'lar. Thought nothing of it.

Mysie Kyle's father took his young ones on instructive folklore expeditions from their home near the Bell o' the Brae at the top of the High Street, where William Wallace faced up to the English.

> He came at them over the wooden Stockwell Bridge and won. My father was keen on Wallace, for we used to go walks out to Wallace's Well at Robroyston where he's supposed to've been hiding in a nearby house when he was given away to the English and taken to London to be hung, drawn and quartered.

They had another lesson, this time in Covenanting history, at the Martyrs' Monument and Well, near the canal.

> That's where the Covenanters Nisbet, Lawson and Wood got put to death. It's all away now. There's just a memorial slab at the Martyr's Church.

Another grisly Glasgow incident has come down through the annals of Janet Kay's family as having been the cause and scene of an unofficial outing of her grandfather's as a youngster.

> He went to see the last public hanging in Glasgow when he was a boy. It was yon Doctor Pritchard who poisoned his wife. He was hanged outside the Glasgow Law-courts and my grandfather and his pals were in the crowd. Nob'dy at home knew where they were.

There's no word of what retribution followed that little adventure but it surely can't have been worse warning than the sight of what society did to bigger-time sinners.

There are not so many now who can remember the very early Glasgow Exhibitions as pictured for a previous volume of memories. But the one in 1938 is as clear to Janet Kay as if fifty-odd years and a Garden Festival had never been.

> What a thing! It was great the Empire Exhibition so it was. Tait's Tower. I remember going up it in a hoist, then walking down. It was a long walk down. And yon coloured fountains all lit up at night. My!

It's not the mighty Palaces of Art and Engineering, the Empire Pavilions or the erudite historical displays that Struan Yule recalls.

> I remember the Laughing Sailor, a sort of dummy that laughed all the time . . . just shook with mirth. And I remember seeing Sir Thomas Lithgow there, very trim in his bowler hat.

He doesn't say why these two should come into his mind together unless ship-builder and laughing mariner had the sea to connect them. Also dressed in a sailor suit, was the Stratosphere Girl, spotlit and visible from all over the Exhibition, performing acrobatics on her swaying pole . . . a favourite memory tinged with sadness over her death not long after 1938 in a fall from her dangerous perch. There are other memories too . . . the 'automatic' chippery where, for tuppence, a poke of vinegared chips came scooshing at you down a chute . . . the Scenic Railway and the wee buggies that shunted you round from place to place when you'd paid your shilling at the Exhibition turnstyle.

Away now from officially organised fun, Agnes Grove recalls early family picnics . . .

> . . . along the canal banks. Must've walked miles out to what's Easterhouse now, with the baby in the pushchair. Instead of taking them to the pictures or that, I had a table-cloth and a kettle with a cap to its stroup, sangwidges and cakes and a primus stove . . . aye, away along the canal.

When the Grove family had served its apprenticeship as well-organised local picnickers, they became flabbergastingly ambitious.

> We went cycling as a family. It all started when Pop bought a tandem. Agnes (my daughter Agnes) shared the tandem with him and he got a seat fixed to the back of my bike for young Arthur. We'd a tent of course and Pop made a side-car for the tandem and put the tent and pots and pans in it.

With this Heath Robinson outfit they were off.

> We'd maybe go to Burntisland and stay overnight at Kincardine on the way . . . put up the tent for the night or the week-end. We were a sight to behold! Then we'd drum up.

The screw-top stroup and the old primus were still in service.

> Drumming up was just brewing up, with the water that we'd carried in the kettle. And we used to meet up with other regulars . . . there was Grandpa Grove and his friends Mr. Caldwell and Mr. Johnston and other folks. Some called the whole bunch the O.M.C.C. . . . the Old Men's Cycling Club. But it wasn't really a club. It was just us.

Burntisland wasn't the only destination. There was the west to be explored as well.

> Sometimes we cycled to Saltcoats from Alexandra Parade. Och, it was maybe good for our lungs and heart . . . but it fairly told on our legs. Mind you, Grandpa Grove went on at the cycling till he was over seventy.

And that in a day when seventy really was three-score-years-and-ten and more than that said to be 'labour-and-sorrow'. Mrs. Duffy-next-door looked after the family dog during these excursions and he had to be restrained from over enthusiastic welcome when they arrived home.

> He would have knocked us down the stair. We were carrying the tandem and the bikes up to the lobby. They were kept there. Three stairs up mind.

Outings there were a-plenty, forbye parties, pantomines and picnics. There were 'the pictures' and to a more 'artistic' extent the theatre. But since the whole culture of Glasgow as Cinema and Repertory city is a subject in itself, it's perhaps best to hang 'outings' on the hook and reminisce about more formal entertainment and maybe 'the dancin' in another chapter.

10

When Buttons were for Sewing On

There's a myth that the housewife of the 1990s has it easy . . . that because washing and ironing, heating, cooking and polishing are done by flicking switches, shaking clothes into shape, opening packets and dipping the family silver into magic liquids, she lives the life of Reilly. She is, it's true, familiar with a plethora of knobs and shortcuts, but on the whole they serve only to release her to do a dozen things her granny never did. There's her share of the working week in office, classroom or shop. There are the committees for the relief of a long list of ills unnamed in older times but that can now be cured or alleviated . . . and the miles she runs up on the car dial to shop for elderly relatives.

All the same she might find her weekly round a dawdle compared with the hassle of rearing six or seven children on a single income, in two rooms if she was lucky, and three if she was bien. Beyond three, she'd probably have had a maid, but still a multitude of other chores to do. All this is a touch simplistic perhaps, for there were cushioned women then, as there are those hard-pressed now, whose lives are the drearier for seeing their sisters with every buyable gadget under the sun. But we are reminiscing here and those who offer their recollections are looking back on years when every hour of the day was given over to putting the clan out clean, well-fed and clothed, and making a tight budget stretch around its weekly needs. Maybe rose-coloured spectacles were issued with clean semmits, for no shiftless, lazy mothers are remembered here. One and all they are recalled as skilled economists and managers. There must have been aimiable sluts, but there was a tightness, a keeping-up with the Tamsons, about tenement life that made it difficult to neglect duty altogether.

> There was a right rammy if the stair didnae get done, and Mistress Whoever got a roasting off the rest up the close.

Today's house-person can choose whether to wash on Friday, do the brasses Monday or Wednesday . . . or even whether to clean the front doorstep at all. There was no such flexi-time or eesie-ose in the rigid order of the closes.

> Yous had your day for this and your day for that. And yous had to stick to them, or else there'd be murder . . . ever'thing out of kilter . . . big rammies.

Of all the rituals brought to mind by those who knew that life in the early century, those to do with the week's laundry are best remembered. Jimmy Dewar was part of that.

> We'd one day a week in the wash-house. It was my job to do the fire under the boiler . . . lit about six in the morning. Then my mother went down. There was a big-big tub and a wooden paddle and the Fell's Naphtha soap. The whites got boiled and stirred, then a wee bit Dolly blue, twice through the wringer and out on the line. When it was just about coming on dry you took it to an old lady along the street who took in mangling and did a load for about tuppence. Sometimes I got to caw the handle. That was a kind of treat.

The wash-house ritual was the same for most, though some like Agnes Grove's mother, before the turn of the century, favoured Reckitt's blue over Dolly and a big spirtle instead of the paddle, and maybe A.1. powder rather than Fell's Naphtha.

> We'd a dumper too, like a big zinc bell on a pole, and you dumped your clo'es with that . . . got up a rare sapple. Then it was all sined a couple of times and your blankets or sheets or that, went to the mangle-wife for flattening and folding. You couldn't iron them if they were too big, y'see. The mangle was the thing, so the laundry didn't get put away all bumphlie.

Indeed Eileen Duffy's mother went into a wee business enterprise with her mangle.

But it was heavy work . . . she couldn't manage, so she didn't keep it long.

Perhaps she hadn't quite the guile that shrewder manglers had, who conned youngsters into believing that it was a big treat to get turning the handle. Agnes Grove was one such willing dupe.

I used to get working the mangle. It had a long wide linen strip you put your clo'es on, and the whole thing went through rollers two or three times as you cawed.

Another who invested in a mangle was a granny in Main Street Bridgeton.

> She did a lot of wee things to get a bit of extra money. She made toffee and she did mending and stitching for ladies. She got hold of a second-hand mangle and got tuppence-a-pair of sheets doing that . . . went out cleaning twice't a week too, and she liked that.

Sometimes a hard-pressed woman went on a wash-house night-shift.

> Mrs. Corrigan up our close done her washing at night. She was out working to some woman and couldnae do it in the day. I used to watch her from the window working with candles lit and the steam comin' out the door across the kin'a whippering light of the candle.

There were few tenement blocks without a wash-house neatly tucked into the corner of the back-court. However weel-kent to those who used it, what it *was* wasn't clear to everyone. Mrs. Mysie Kyle recalls . . .

> I remember reading about a delegation of Russian visitors to Glasgow who went home and wrote up articles about the Glasgow tenements with wee-wee houses built in behind them.

Maybe they saw them as Granny or 'Babushka' annexes, or just for the tenements' overspill.

> Yes, they thought, what with the fires and chimneys, the windows and the door, and likely a pram sitting outside, it must've been a house. (The prams were for carting the washing, of course.)

Everyone had big washings to do, but the young housewives Christina and her sister Mary, struggling at Maclean Street, had more than their fair share.

> There was always some of our brothers coming home from sea. Not to help . . . oh no! They didn't know the dairy work or that. They just brought more work with them because we'd their bags to sort out and their washing to do. We did that in the wash-house out the back, where the byre and the stable was. Chrissie and I.

If the wash-house facilities were't up to scratch or if you fancied wash-day as more of a social occasion, you could go to the steamie. The Hutchison clothes went to the Pollokshaws steamie.

My sister used to go at six o'clock in the morning and if I was on my holiday from school I went with her. Th'was wee kind of places each. At the side of your sink was your own wee boiler 't you could boil up your things yourself. An'en you took them out and into the big tub and let the water run on them . . . then into your wee tub and you did your wash wi' a board. Yon 'Steamie' on the T.V. was just th'exact real thing . . . awful good! Then you sined the clo'es. (Mind you can go dressed to the steamie now, it's all just machines, but you couldnae then. It was big wellies and a rubber apron, for you got soaked.)

The chummy time of chat with other perspiring women came when you were waiting for the next stage.

What they called a spin drier . . . no' a machine, just a big drum that a man pulled the lever and the brake, and the water came scooshing out. You werenae allowed to touch it. Just the man did that.

A few more bits of local clash and 'the man' was finished.

Then you pulled out a rack from a kin'a cupboard wi' hot pipes running along it, put your clo'es over that and pushed it into the heat again. That was extra mind. But it was all just coppers.

For a likely lad there was another copper or two to be had on steamie day.

My mother-in-law used to do her washing at the one off the Garscube Road, and my husband when he was wee got thruppence for carrying the basket of washing on his head to the steamie and back.

Wash-house or steamie, A.1. or soft soap, one thing was for sure a 'nice washing' got gold stars, and a 'gey grey' one was the kiss of death to respectability.

Then there was the ironing.

It seemed to go on for days. All the petticoats and sheets, the table-cloths and the other clothes. I got doing the hankies sometimes. At first it was flat irons that sat at the front of the range fire . . . different sizes. Later we'd a bolt-iron. You heated the bolt then slid it in through a hole in the back . . . put it in and out with a cleek that had a wee hook on the end.

The next advance on the bolt iron was the smart new gas iron favoured in Janet Kay's home . . . hazardous but trendy.

> We'd a gas point for the gas ring on the range and we could take it off
> and just push the rubber tube on to the iron instead.

The bodies that had to go into these sappled, sined and flat-ironed
sarks and petties, had to be scoured themselves into the cleanliness
that was next to godliness. Much has been related elsewhere of
Friday bath night, so a reminder of such scenes is enough to bring
back a passing picture here.

> Friday nights . . . oh aye . . . your hair 'looked', then your tubbing in
> front of the range in the zinc bath that was kep' hung up behind the
> toilet door. Sometimes when I was bigger we went to the public baths
> and got a good steep. After wir bath, if it was the zinc, all the six of us
> sat in a row along the kitchen bed . . . a' shinin' in wir nightgowns,
> and got a cup i' cocoa.

Even when those angelic young were up and had flown the nest
they sometimes came home for a scrub. Mrs. Mysie Kyle did.

> When I got married we'd no hot water, just a toilet. We went to
> my mother for baths. Other folk went to Townhead baths and for
> a shilling you got your bath and a towel.

Zinc tubbing or shilling steep over, attention could be turned
to surroundings. Priority was what was going to meet the visitor
first or the beady eye of other women in the close, however
intimate.

> Twice in the week you did the stairs. The factor got the upper part
> of the walls white-washed, that was his job. But then you took a
> bit of pipe-clay (whitening y'know). You champed it up then put it
> in the water. When it dissolved you white-washed down the whole
> stair. Some folk just drew designs down the edge instead. Neighbours
> could be quite sniffy if it wasn't done right.

So could grandmothers.

> There was always the stair to do. It was a wally close ours . . . nice
> green and brown tiles, and my grandmother inspected to see you'd
> no wee splashes on the tiles from your pipe-clay. Yes she did. She
> inspected that.

They could have done with Bunty Angles' granny and her eagle
eye in the Andersons' close.

We'd an old woman washed our stair . . . slittered the water all over the place . . . left the close swimming. My father used to call her Mrs. Noah.

The pipe-clay, universally employed as it was to create a trig ambience, had its drawbacks.

There were thirty-six weans up our close all tramping whitening on to their lobby rugs.

The blame for that misfortune might have been laid firmly at the Calton door of Alex Donnelly's father.

In his wee pipe work he made the pipe-clay for the closes, farthing a square.

The state of the brasses was another touchstone for a family's reputation. Outside first.

The door handle and the name-plate and letter-box got brassoed every day and the wee knobs on the bannister that stopped you sliding down.

Granny was on hand to examine those too, and woe betide the slattern who left grey-green smudges round the brass bosses or the post-box. There were some households whose outside-the-front-door duties did not stop at pipe-clay and brasses . . . those who added to their labours the scouring of the stairhead cludgie.

We were in a single-end off of Argyle Street when I was young, and it was my job to clean the cludgie when it came our turn. We shared with the Boyles and the Shaughnessys. I hated that, but it had had to get done twice't a week . . . scrubbed and done wi' Jeyes' Fluid.

Scrubbing was a skill learned young and skinny, when you'd to do almost a limbo dance to get into the places where oose or even the scandal of actual *dirt* might lurk. That granny again, saw to it that her dark corners were clean as a whistle.

She was sixty when I was born and came to live with her . . . well-on to be bringing up a wee one. But she was strict and I had my chores. One was to take everything out from under the Room bed and get in on my hands and knees to scrub the floor. Then you'd to let it dry before the boxes went back.

That press bed space was virtually a bedroom too.

> I slept in there with a shelf above my head and another one above
> my feet for all my clothes. The bed was quite high . . . just a feather
> mattress on top of slats of wood. My grandmother stretched over and
> made the bed with a walking-stick. Oh, she was quick and nimble
> with that stick! And when she turned the mattress she fairly made the
> feathers fly.

Mrs. Dewar of Cartvale Road was another stickler for below-bed
perfection.

> Except for under the rugs and mats that would have slipped, she
> polished all the lino . . . Mansion polish . . . even under the bed
> . . . had to be shining. Spotless, the lino floors were, but awful
> cold.

Whether lino was cold or not, Peggy Carson's mother tossed her
head at the sight of a *carpet* arriving at a neighbour's door.

> When her man won a wee bit money she put down this carpet in her
> kitchen. Ma thought she'd just got above hersel' . . . lazy too, that only
> the surround had to be scrubbed.

While mothers took their smeddum out on the floors, the young
had their tasks.

> I'd to lift all the rugs and take them out to beat on the clothes line down
> the green. Had to do it before 12 noon on a Saturday. There was some
> bye-law or other said that.

No doubt he did that at his busy mother's bidding, but for
the independent young Rodgers in Govan the chores were self
inflicted.

> All the lino'd to be done ev'ry morning. And then it was all white
> wood in our kitchen . . . chairs, dresser, table, shelves, everything
> . . . even the top of the coal bunker. So that had to be scrubbed.

You can't get much spicker or spanner than scrub your coal
bunker. But this, after all, was 'farm' forbye city tenement and
when the scrubbers got round to the press in the corner they often
found reward.

We'd a particular hen in the yard and when the window was opened this hen used to flap up from outside, jump into the sink and then down to the press door that was always a crack open. We'd a piece of woollen cloth there for her and she used to go in on to that and lay an egg. Then she would walk across the floor, out the front door and down the back close to the rest of the hens.

Best recollected of all the home scenes of eighty and ninety years ago, are those surrounding the range. The elderly who basked in its warmth as youngsters and waited for what it delivered to them of soups and scones, look back with nostalgia. Mothers who were slaves to such fires blessed the day it was hacked out of the wall in favour of a prissy turn-off gas cooker. Janet Kay's memories take her round her granny's kitchen before coming to rest on the range.

There was the dresser with cupboards above, then round to a single window with a black sink under it . . . and then the kitchen press for dishes and food. Then there was the range. My granny's range was very old . . . no polished trims and just the black kerb. In our own house the hearth was white enamel with flowers and there was a polished towel-rail right across the top. My granny's had no shiny bits.

But the Hutchisons' 'shiny bits' were their pride and joy. Ann Hutchison . . .

My, our range was beautiful! My Daddy kept it lovely. That was always his job. You know the steel bit at the front? Daddy had it beautiful. Did it with emery. And he'd the doors an' that black-leaded. We heated all our water on that range. The kettles were on the boil all the time.

Jimmy Dewar recalls the emery-and-zebo treatment.

I loved that range. I did the emery paper all round the steel bits. I'd be maybe ten or eleven. Mother did the black-leading, and buffing with a velvet pad. The range had a black fender with wee low lumpy pillars at the corners. Mother baked cakes in the oven and oatcakes on the big girdle on the top. She'd a gas ring too that was hinged to lift out the way when she was using the top of the range.

A dozing eavesdropper suddenly open his eyes to recall theirs . . .

. . . had burnished steel that you did with a wee pad with two rings on it for your fingers and close metal coils for the rubbing. There was a wee shelf in front of the fire ribs with a grid you could pull up and slip your oatcakes in to dry out.

Your mother might be from Tuscany but, once a Glasgow housewife, she had to master her range . . . and her Scottish weans. Mario Servadei's mother did both.

We'd all our household chores. Yes the boys in Italian families had to take their share. I'd the brasses to do and the range . . . the Zebo and the steel bits. And I'd to chop up the sticks on freezing cold mornings.

The range in Mrs. Mysie Kyle's early married home had the usual steel rims but was unique in another way.

Y'know someone had *painted* that range, and they'd done a good job on it, so it wasn't nearly the work. I never had to black-lead that grate all the time I was there . . . just emery the edges.

Girdle scones and stews, dumplings and oven baking came out of Glasgow's ranges in a steady stream. Only a prodigal woman admitted to using 'bought cakes' and maybe only a hard-pressed one had to resort to cooking what she called 'buff'.

Our charlady used to tell us about cooking buff. It was the lungs of an animal. 'You just hook the thrapple over the edge of the pot,' she used to say, 'and the rest of it gets boiled. Then it gets cut up and eaten. Fair fills them a' up'.

Coal for the range, kept in the kitchen bunker, was a big item on a tight budget, but there were what some called 'savers' and others 'briquettes' and there were other fly wee ways of making the coal spin out. There were fire-bricks you could put at each side or maybe an iron nest in the middle, to take up space. And there were also local resources.

That same charwoman that cooked the buff lived in Kinning Park, beside a big ash-covered area of waste ground, and she said people used to send their children out after dark with buckets to bring back cinders for the range.

Wherever the fuel came from, there was a set pattern for the fire chore.

> You put on your dust cap and your thibbet apron, picked out the big cinders, cleeked the ashes forward and put them in a baikie to take down the back. Then you made the fire.

Ranges were treated with, if not always *loving* care, at least with respect by most folk, for they could be stubborn. But there were the cavaliers.

> People used to put their chimneys on fire . . . to save the sweep. Put the whole close in danger that.

There was another feature of houses around 1905 that might have sent the close up in flames.

> It was gas light we had, you turned up the screw and put a taper to it . . . just the naked flame.

In Janet Kay's home the arrangements were not so primitive.

> Oh yes, gas lights. They had swan neck fitments, wide brackets and glass bowls, and mantles that you lit with a taper. Veritas mantles . . . a wee white net thing with a pipe-clay ring round it. I can smell them yet. You'd to kind of 'prove' the mantles with a taper to get the waxiness off them.

Even safer, if less mellow, illumination was on the way.

> I remember when we got the electric. The factor lived in our street so maybe that's why we got it so early in the twenties. They only laid quite a small cable in Cartvale Road because they thought it was a flash in the pan and not very many would want the electric. It cost seven pounds to wire the whole house and put up the fittings.

As well as those old glowing ranges that were at the very heart of home and memory, there was another set-piece that took a worthy woman hours of work to have to her satisfaction.

> My granny slept in the kitchen. The bed was in the wall on bierers, a frame of slats laid on wooden legs that held up the mattress. You took them with you when you flitted mind. Then th'was a front board and over that hung the bed poinds. That was crocheted lace points

on a white insertion, a kind of valance really. Then th'was always a white-white bedspread. Later when you got coloured spreads you'd still always a white one for when the doctor came. Then th'were pillow shams with nothing in them. They'd goffered frills that my mother stood for hours with a goffering iron to get the rucks just right. It was like Marcel waving, so it was (D'you mind of Marcel waving for your hair?) Your wall bed *had* to be just so, because your friends and neighbours came right into the kitchen. I remember too that Granny had a weaver's kist beside her bed that she used for blankets. Th'was a wee drawer in it too where the weaver had kept his bobbins. I used to sit on that kist.

The polished black kettle with the marble in it against 'furring', the glowing range, the brasses and the cludgie, the weekly bath, the hair hunt, these were Friday night operations in most families, but in Jewish households, like Mrs. Lily Joseph's, Thursday was the big night.

We'd a samovar for making our tea . . . a brass samovar my parents had brought with them when they came from Russia. It got polished with the other brasses on a Thursday night. And I can always remember the six silver dish-covers all shined up. The range got done and all the dishes ready. We'd different dishes for different things. We were very Orthodox and at Passover you'd a different set altogether for everything. Anyway, it had all to be ready for Friday, the very special Friday dinner. By the Friday at one o'clock everything was done and we'd a non-Jewish fireboy in to get the range going for us. We got home early from school on winter Fridays to be ready before dark.

Come the Friday night all was ready.

Never less than twelve of us sat down at the big kitchen table and we'd always strangers sat down with us. There'd be two or three soups, chicken maybe, or broth or cabbage. We weren't flush with money but never short. Mother was a great cook, learned it from their housekeeper back in Russia. We'd all the Orthodox rituals like in the Bible, the candles and all that, and the right things that were read and said.

So tenement families, whether Glasgow-born for generations or immigrants from less hospitable places, learned to hone their household skills and economies early. Perhaps the first sign of becoming part of the more effete, upwardly mobile society was to acquire a maid.

> I was a lazy wee snob. I hated Molly's half-day, because I'd to lay the table, go to the kitchen with dirty plates or whatever . . . and then *wash-up*. Then the war came and put the kybosh on the maids. They all went home and into war work. That was as big a shock to me at twelve, as the British Expeditionary Forces going to France.

> Oh yes, I had a maid. I had a wee brass bell at the tea-table to summon Agnes in her afternoon pinny, cuffs and black dress. She'd fetch and carry between kitchen and table, then take her own through there by herself. And of course she'd always a lot of housework while I was maybe out in the town. Terrible when you think on it now.

There's a thowlessness about families being waited on hand and foot that does seem objectionable in the 1990s . . . almost feudal. But one who did the running after, and answered the table bell or the front door, sees another side to it all.

> I left home at sixteen and into service and y'know, when th'was a lot of unemployment and you'd a house burstin' wi' weans and mibbe two or three wi' T.B., then a place in a nice house, wi' a garden p'raps, your ain warm room, good meals and your keep, wi' a wee bit money in your pocket on your half day . . . plus something to send home, it didnae seem that bad . . . and you often got quite nice clo'es off of the mistress. Eighteen shillings a month I got in the early 1920s.

However much maids or mothers or tenement children had to do to keep families clean, warm, fed and solvent, few could have had the additional duties that fell to the household in McLean Street.

> With my father being an invalid and Maw gone and the shop and the farm there . . . we'd a lot of chores, scrubbing and washing and ironing . . . *and* the cows, the chickens and the dairy.

And that wasn't all.

> The boys got off with it away at sea. When I was young one of them left me with his doos. And I got what-for if anything went wrong with one of them, I can tell you.

Sometimes there was even a little veterinary work.

> When a hen got the croup . . . you should've heard a hen wi' the croup,

going ooo–ooo–ooo! What a noise! I used to say to Papa (always called him Papa, Mother was Maw) 'Papa, that hen's got the croup'. And he would lift her in a bag and I would make wee balls of fresh butter and roll it in pepper. Then Papa would open the beak and put about six of these down the hen's thrapple. That seemed to work great.

All that then, was the domestic way of it, in the days when coal had to be dragged up three stairs, washday started at six in the morning, and buttons were for sewing on, and not just pressing to magic housework away.

11

Annaker's Sausages are the Best

Since an ancient pedlar first laid out his wares one fine day on a grass track verge and, for the good weather and honest prices, called the pitch a 'fair', bartering, comparing and selecting have added up to shopping as one of man's favourite activities. For these pages there was no exhaustive list of where this or that emporium was sited, just a random mulling over of recollected counters and encounters. And yet there emerged memories of almost the entire range of household and personal merchandise . . . from clothing to china, butcher to bakery, furniture to fish, ironmongery, the gamut of grocery to haberdashery, tobacco and flowers. And best remembered of all, the joys of cheuch-jean, sherbet-dab and buttermilk dainty.

Take the big stores first. Upmarket, downmarket, between market, each had its own specialty, each its own circle of customers, and only in a determined hunt for something elusive did the clientèle of one overlap another.

> Oh there was nothing like Sauchiehall Street for elegant ladies, maybe up to about the 1930s! They'd their choice of a dozen or more big shops. They all sold everything in the way of clothes, but had their own different specialties too. Daly's was very chic for gowns and beautiful coats. Copland's was school things and gloves . . . for the gloves you leant your elbow on a wee cushion, hand straight up, and the assistant drew them on finger by finger.

Gracious days indeed with the only sounds the low hum of discreet conversation between assistant and shopper or the soft 'woosh' of money being conveyed by tube to the counting-house.

That used to intrigue me when the money was sent up yon tube-thing for change, screwed into a wee container.

One who operated that mechanism, no doubt in all the dignity of black jacket and striped trouser, remembers a less formal use for the tube and claims to have caused pandemonium in the cash-office by putting a live mouse he had caught into the tube and sending it off.

Pettigrew's had its following too.

They'd lovely material and good quality school clothes, and they'd a small orchestra in the tea-room too. Henderson's was just general . . . nice though. There was Forsyths' too and the likes of Rowan's and

Fraser's, and Simpson, Hunter and Young in Buchanan Street. Some
preferred it down there, but for a real afternoon out I liked Sauchiehall
Street.

At a time when Glasgow to outsiders was 'shipyards and slums',
discerning local women were well aware that it was also a fine
shopping centre, second to none, and certainly not to its rival in
the east.

> I can remember my mother meeting an Edinburgh lady on holiday
> and-here this lady asked her if she never came to Edinburgh to shop!
> Go to Edinburgh to shop? With Sauchiehall Street and Buchanan
> Street on her doorstep. Edinburgh . . . sight-see maybe. Shopping
> . . . never!

There were those passing mentions of Buchanan Street and
some loyalists would have gone no further than the majestic
stairway, galleries and stately ambience of Wylie and Lochhead;
the refinement of Macdonald's, sober, tailored Rowan's; even the
more popular bustle of Fraser's and Wyllie Hill's. But it is the
big-store names in Sauchiehall Street that trip most readily off
elderly Glasgow tongues. Mrs. Millicent Davis, now of Dunblane,
is quite adamant that things have not improved.

> I like to remember Glasgow as it was in the days before the demise
> of Pettigrew and Stephen's, Copland and Lye and Daly's. There's
> nothing comparable now. I remember Daly's with the real Willow
> Tearoom. It was just delightful.

Occasionally, perhaps with a friend who was a Pettigrew's
devotee, or in the days when she went where she was taken,
as a child . . .

> I used to go for tea at Pettigrew's. It was decorated in pale grey
> and their china was *gorgeous* . . . grey lattice designs with pink
> flowers.

And people used to beat a pathway to the Aladdin's basement at
Trèron et Cie (where someone claims to have once had Mr. Cie*
pointed out to her!)

*et cie – and Company

It was the china . . . oh my, that china! A whole hall of it there
was. It was a good shop all over, but it was best known for all
the different makes of china . . . the Spode and the Doulton and
the Wedgwood, and just the old 'Blue Dawn' and Meekin's using-
wally.

The dainty Trèron tearoom upstairs is recalled as another feature.

There was a quartet played music and they'd always posies of flowers
and silver cake-stands on the table. Once I remember we must have
been sitting there near closing time and the waitress (y'know, in nice
black dress and white pinny and cap) came over and was going to take
away the flowers.
   But Mamma said 'Excuse me, but could you leave the flowers till
we're finished please. We're enjoying them so much'. and so we
were.

Come August though, when it was down-to-earth shopping for
the winter under-duds and working gear, good, plain, middle-
priced Paisley's in Jamaica Street was the place.

Paisley's was all kinds of uniforms and work clothes like overalls and
boiler-suits . . . and maids' wrappers and pinnies, and of course for
your combinations and liberty bodices.

An elderly lady still smarts at what she sees as her family's
chauvinistic excursions to Paisley's.

I got taken for my Chilprufe combinations and pinafores. It wasn't so
much the pinafores but I couldnae thole the combies . . . or the ribbed
stockings held up on yon suspenders that buttoned on to your liberties.
I'm sayin' *held up* but they crinkled round your knees and you'd a big
gape at the back you'd to keep hitching up. But my brother! Oh, he
got his kilt and all his orders, silver button jacket, tartan socks . . .
standing there quite jokoh in his Balmoral with the red toorie . . .
and a dirk for his sock. He got a *dirk* . . . and I got combies! That was
Paisley's.

And it still rankles after eighty years. Furniture stores too had their
social layers, from the sedate exclusiveness of Gardner's and Wylie
and Lochhead to the more modest 'Bows-of-the-High-Street' and
Wyllie Hill's and even a turn-of-the century one opposite Boot's
Corner, that Jack Roche remembers.

An uncle of mine used to work at that Glasgow Bedding and Bedstead Centre on the same side as the Hielan'man's Umbrella. That would've been eighty years ago and I remember seeing women working at the mattresses.

Those were the places that the discerning, quality-rather-than-bargain folk spent their solid budgets and where the polished brass facings to their deep window-sills were unhooked at night and taken inside for safe-keeping. Most families being 'wage' rather than 'salary' earning, couldn't always afford the economics of the 'good thing' that would last for years, and found that other emporia (or even the Barras) suited their purses better.

Th'was Dallas's and the Colosseum and Arnott Simpson's, quite good serviceable clo'es you got there, but not the kind of cut and quality of the other places. I went there a lot for clo'es and at the Colosseum you could get a three-course lunch and a cup of tea for 1/9. That would be the late twenties. They were good for towels and sheets and things. Bow's and the 'Poly' were good bargain places too. And sometimes, maybe before the First War, my mother went to the Bonanza in George Square if things were a bit tight for my father.

They knew their stores, those thrifty ladies, and their stores knew them.

They're great nowadays for their 'market research', but in the big stores, where I worked long before it was heard of, we knew fine what it was all about.

And the long-retired employee of one such store shakes a knowing head over modern arty lay-outs and packaged, untouchable stock.

It's a mistake . . . your wee Glasgow body likes a good rummage.

Many a good rake in the likes of Dallas's is remembered by those with quite slender purses. But there were other well-doing folk even harder put to it to present a bien appearance, even if they weren't all as badly off as those who resorted to the pawn-shop.

When you were skint your father's Sunday clo'es went into the pawn, but that was quite good forbye the wee bit money, because when you'd no cupboards or wardrobes your things got hung up and looked after till you wanted them the next Sunday.

The Hutchison family were not pawners but still hard-put-to-it to present the bien appearance they managed to keep up.

My Daddy had a big family to manage, and my Mother dead. When we were nearly grown-up we got half-a-crown a week . . . and that was for everything. You'd to buy all your clo'es out of that. My sister Jeanie didn't get much either to keep the house and see to the five boys. She really brought us all up. We didn't go up the town often, except if you'd something big you needed.

For Mrs. Chrissie Ronnie too, a trip into the town was a rare treat.

I was away in service and I wasn't home often, but when I was, I used to go in to look at the windows or, say, buy a vest. That would maybe be 1s.11½d. And if you'd only 1s.11d well, you didnae get it. My wages then, in the early twenties, were never over £2 a month.

Sometimes a visit to town was for service rather than goods. Joe

Harper lifting his head from a game of Senior Citizen dominoes, recalls Boot's Corner as it used to be.

> Th'was this big tobacconist's long ago (I'm talking maybe 1908 or 1909) and you could see from the top of the tram SMOKE HOWELL'S TOBACCOS on its shop blind. Then above that th'was Cherry's Shaving Parlour and brush-up place with an advertisement black painted on the wall for THE MOST HYGIENIC HAIR BRUSHING MACHINE IN GLASGOW. You could get your boots polished there an' all. All that was below a hotel on the next storey . . . maybe the old Adelphi . . . or maybe it had some other name before that.

Those blind and wall-stencilled adverts were an extension of the centuries-old hanging signs.

> The shops used to all have signs set up to hang outside them. I s'pose originally for them that couldnae read . . . but I'm talking maybe seventy-eighty year ago. Usually they were on hinges or wee rings and you could hear them creakin' in the wind. There would be a big haddie or-that outside the fishmonger . . . and mortars and pestles at the chemist. And I mind a lum hat outside a gents' shop . . . and the barber's pole, of course . . . and was there no' a yellow and green cow at the Buttercup or some other dairy?

Jack Roche recalls a sign on the southside, or at least hearing about it.

> My grandpa used to talk about a pub sign in Strathbungo that was a cut-out head of Robert Burns . . . no' very like him, he said (how he could tell that I don't know). But there was quite a lot of Burns connections in that area wi' Burns' daughter by Anna Park livin' there. She's buried out at Pollokshaws. Her son was brought up there and he wrote poems too.

That southside pub brings us away from the city where the department stores, however grand or modest, were for all-day excursions, with tea and a slice of Craig's fruit loaf or Fuller's walnut cake thrown in. From such establishments a face or figure may sometimes be remembered . . . a Tartar at the Outsize Dresses or a wing-collared shop-walker pacing a stately beat among the counters. But the warmest and most human memories are not those of the big stores, they're rather of the corner shops where Maggie Brodie or Charlie Nolan cut your ham to your precise thickness, or trusted you with half-a-pound of cheese till pay-poke day, and where the surroundings were as familiar as your own front room.

> I mind a nice grocer's in Dennistoun . . . wi' all wee polished drawers for lentils or peas or that, and the names of what was in them on the outside, under kind of crystal handles. Th'was sacks of grain and potatoes, big brass scales and a marble counter . . . and celluloid black and white price tickets stuck in the cheeses. Th'was big black, what they called 'Japan', tins for different teas, and a biscuit rack with big containers that had hinged lids to get at the biscuits, it was always loose biscuits then.

And at the East Kilbride Dairy in the early thirties you got red pencil-sharpeners with Youma bread, from Miss King.

> . . . remember Youma bread? Yon were nice pencil-sharpeners, and in the chemist you got a board game with toothpaste . . . that was the Ivory Castle game, all about Giant Decay, for good children that brushed their teeth.

Not that your actual *shop* was always the place to go for messages. Jimmy Dewar remembers the buying and selling that went on out at Hogganfield.

> There was an interesting small holding there, maybe about five or six acres. Pinkerton's Rhubarb Farm. I used to see all the work people out in the summer picking rhubarb . . . famous place was Pinkerton's. Next door to the grocers I worked for at Battlefield was a fruit and veg shop owned by a Mrs. Pinkerton. I wondered if she belonged to that same family.

Jewish children often had interesting and exotic errands.

> I can remember when we lived in Stockwell Street I used to go with my mother to buy fish at the Clydeside, where the *Carrick* sailing-ship was for a long time. Often on a Friday they'd sell you a big parcel of fish . . . cod mostly. She'd cook it in milk and it was delicious. You got those cheap parcels of fish at the fish market too.

There were Jewish shops too, and Lily Balarsky remembers those.

They were mostly just across the bridge. I remember some of the old Jewish shopkeepers . . . yes . . . with long beards. Mr. Greenberg had a delicatessen and Mother used to send me for messages and of course she hadn't learned to speak English properly. There was a grain, a pin-head oatmeal that she used as a base for soup, but she didn't know the English name for it and she would send me across the Stockwell Bridge to this man's place for a pound of 'hoberni gropen' . . . it's groats really. That's the Yiddish name, and I was all embarrassed and crying at having to go. Says-I, wailing, 'But I need to know the right name'. And she says 'you just go and ask for "hoberni gropen", *he'll* know'. And right-enough the man knew fine what I wanted.

Sometimes the fish too was from Mr. Greenberg rather than the Clyde quay.

He'd big barrels of salt herrings outside the door, real salt herring. And he used to lift it out dripping on to the scales, then into a newspaper. There were a lot of 'deli' and fruit shops there in the Gorbals, and Jewish butchers where you got wurst and so on. The meat was kosher, butchered on the same principle as the 'halal' . . . the traditional religious customs from the hot climate in the Middle East. Still done of course, but if I'm a bit nostalgic it's because my memories are warm of that time, and you've got to say it the way it was. Otherwise there's no real truth.

Vivid pictures from seventy or more years ago can be dredged up even from something as insubstantial as remembered smell. Mr. Edward Aldington sees a Tollcross dairy.

I used to be sent from Mount Vernon to a dairy in Tollcross for butter. You stepped down into the shop and it had a rough slabbed floor with barrels and with cans of milk on it. And there was always this slightly *sour* smell hanging about. I've always remembered that.

Sometimes a rememberer himself was part of the mellow scene in an old shop . . . like the late Mr. James McClelland.

I was a grocery boy my first job. In the east end. I took the deliveries of course, but there were other things you'd to do. I did the sawdust . . . wetting it to sweep up, then put fresh stuff down. I can still smell that new sawdust and the potatoes I unloaded into a big open-fronted bunker. Another job was shovelling them out into quarter stones.

Maybe seventy years from now people will yearn when they remember the obstinate set of supermarket trolley wheels, or the thrill of lifting down a packet of biscuits from among a thousand others tasting much the same, or even the plastic spacemen they got free with their cornflakes. Maybe there'll be the same nostalgic sparkle for the slimy feel of pre-packed bacon as lights up elderly faces now when the bakers or butchers of their greenstick years are recalled.

> I used to get sent to this butcher in Crosshill. There was a shelf for all the hams . . . Belfast, Wiltshire, Ayrshire. You chose what you wanted, then I always remember a wee thing he did. He always took his knife up the cutting end of the roll of bacon as if he was brushing up the fibres or the grain or something. We bought cuts for soup too or maybe a sheep's head. Shops were open till all hours then and the only light in that butcher's was gas . . . jets all round the shop. No mantles, just raw sort of spade-shaped flames. I think they were called butterfly or fish-tail jets. And then of course there was always water trickling down the windows to help keep things fresh.
>
> I used to put my tongue to the window for a wee drink, thinking the water was outside.

The Dewars' butcher was quite a novelty in her day, for she was what old gravestones call a 'relict'.

> We'd this lady butcher. Her husband had been killed in the First War, maybe about 1915. She carried on the shop. What a talker! You went in for three quarters of mince . . . took you about an hour. That was Maggie Graham. There was another butcher that sold mince at sixpence a pound. My mother thought it was rubbish at sixpence instead of maybe ninepence at Maggie Graham's.

Sometimes a shop was one of a small chain around the city's outskirts. Peggy Carson recalls a well-known name that has long passed into proverb.

> We used to talk about someb'dy's house being like Annacker's midden. Annacker had butcher's shops . . . made sausages . . . so I s'pose his bins at the back would be messy. Mind, I used to wonder if his name really was Annacker right-enough, or if he just called himself that and it was really *a knacker's* midden . . . but that's just my own wee idea.

But Mrs. Bunty Angles shakes her head at such blasphemy and rummages for a photograph.

> No, no. Here's a picture of the shop with his name quite clear at the top. See . . . William Annacker. There was rivalry y'know, between Annacker's sausages and Waddell's of Napiershall Street, and there was a wee rhyme.
> Annacker's sausages are the best
> In your belly they do rest
> Waddell's sausages are the wurst
> In your belly they do burst.

McGonagall rather than Tennyson, but the message is clear. Peggy Carson has the last word though on her suspicions of the old name.

> Could've been just a made-up shop name. There are no Annackers in the 'phone book now, sure there aren't?

There was the Co-op too. The Co. did well for those who were loyal to it and cocked a snook at those who looked down on it.

> My mother was black-affronted once when someone saw only half of the back door of Cooper's van outside our house . . . didn't see the 'er's . . . and said to her, 'didn't know you dealt with the Co-op, Mistress Hunter'.

But Lily Balarsky's mother took a different view.

> Great thing the Co-op. My mother shopped there a lot. I can remember her number even yet . . . 23930. You used to get stamps you saved up and got your 'divvy' every year. It was great for working people. My mother once got a holiday through the Co-op.

Co-op numbers are branded into many an elderly Glasgow mind . . . 63450, 4075, 63785 . . . a dozen rememberers rattled them off. Mrs. Nell Dinsmor recalls her mother's Co-op days at Barrhead.

> 4114 was her number. Och, the Co. was an institution . . . in the middle of Barrhead. That was the big Co-op for all over . . . the whole kaboodle, the bakery and the big-big laundry. The bakery was a marvellous place. Before the New Year your mother mixed her Ne'erday bun and I got to carry it to the bakehouse to get it baked there for thruppence or sixpence, depending on the size. And they'd

horse-drawn vans that went round selling. On Fridays the specialty
was meat pies. The steam fairly came fleeing out the van because all
the stuff was put in hot. Another specialty was what we called Cat's
Faces. a sort of cookie in stuck-together sections with sugar on the top.
That was a real treat.

The lady who was mortified at the idea of taking her custom to the
Co. had an altogether more remote relationship with her grocer.

It was Cooper's of Howard Street we dealt with. They phoned for
the order, then the groceries would be delivered in a big square
coffee-coloured van the next day. Sometimes you paid by post, but
sometimes you went into town to pay the account. I remember the
lovely smells of coffee and ham. It was quite a dark shop I remember,
but kind of 'classy'. Not so posh though as Manuel and Webster's. My
friend went there, but I was like my mother, just a wee bit too thrifty
for that.

Morning shopping was for groceries, but when you'd had
your dinner (in early-century Glasgow almost invariably at
midday) there was other local shopping to be done. There
might be darning needles, buttons, hair ribbons, or wool for
the interminable knitting of socks and stockings. There was a
wee draper-cum-shoe shop in the Carsons' street before the First
War.

It was an old lady had it, a wee lady *overflowing* with fat. She'd black
woollen stockings and flat, strap-and-button shoes. One side the shop
was yarns and knitting pins, stockings and corsets, on the other side she
sold laces and speckled sandshoes along wi' the boots and shoes. For
them you sat with your feet on a sloping box and if it was button boots
she tweaked them through wi' a wee button-hook. It just twinkled up
the row of buttons.

After all the worthy purchases your mother made when you
were young if you were lucky and there was a copper or two left
you had your own precious income to lay out on luxuries.

Friday night was Band of Hope night and you'd your penny to spend.
It was the done thing on your way there to go into Birrell's and buy
Russian toffees.
  Ogo-pogo eyes were the great thing wi' us. You sooked them fae
one colour to another, yellow, pink, blue, green . . . maybe five or

six different colours. You'd to keep takin' them out your mouth . . .
to make sure you werenae missing a colour.

Soor plooms, spearmint chews, X.L. chewing gum, aniseed balls,
midget gems . . . all had their following, but Jack Roche preferred
quality to quantity.

> My favourite was yon FIVE BOYS chocolate, with the row of wee
> boys' faces on the front. The first one was crying and miserable, then
> each one after that was a bit more cheerful. What were the words under
> them . . . DESPERATION, PACIFICATION, EXPECTATION,
> ACCLAMATION, REALISATION.

> It's sherbet dabs I mind of the best. You licked the sherbet off a wee flat
> stick or sooked it through a liquorice tube. We'd cinnamon sticks that
> we chewed and we made sugarollie water. You just shook your hard
> liquorice in a bottle of water. It was s'posed to go darker and better if
> you did it under the bed.

Mary Rodger was a sugarollie-water-maker.

> If you'd a ha'penny you bought liquorice, long ropes of it. You could
> eat it or make sugarollie water. Or you maybe bought caramels. I was
> awful fond of caramels.

Her sister Chrissie preferred tiger nuts.

> You got an awful lot for a ha'penny and chewed them. They were
> like wee hard raisins.

All these would be bought in small shops around the home streets
of their customers, but north of the city there was a Mecca for
connoiseurs from all airts, like the Morton family.

> There was Skene's shop up Alexandra Parade at Castle Street where
> the white tram and the red tram stopped. There were queues there on a
> Saturday night for their sweeties. Skene's was a famous sweetie shop.

Of course there were always expansive souls who preferred
fleeting pleasure to the long investment in sucking or chewing.

> The first time I'd real money in my pocket I went in and had a peach
> melba. What an extravagance! But it was good.

Ice-cream fanciers had almost the whole Italian immigrant

population of the city providing for their samplings and comparisons, and rememberers are still fiercely certain that their own local 'Tally' had the secret of the perfect recipe. 'Tally'? Perhaps there are still Italians who bridle at that term, but the genial restaurateur reminiscing for this book is not one of them.

> Used to it. In the old days they didn't like it. But it's just a sort of term of affection now. I think 'Paki' will get to be like that too, that's the way most people use it . . . kind of friendly. And when the Pakistanis get to know the Glasgow folk better, the feeling of being offended'll pass. I hope so. They're nice people.

The final forlorn word on sweets and similar treats must go to Robert Ford who is one of the few not to have a list of old-time favourites.

> Got no pennies, nothing like that. You didn't get much sweeties.

Later years have been kinder to Mr. Robert Ford than they were to the young Bobby and he can now enjoy (the better perhaps for sparse times in childhood) the pleasures of the purchase that other rememberers knew in the days of seventy, eighty, ninety years ago when they bartered with Mr. Greenberg or Mr. Cie.

12
Ladies from Hell

The wars of this century have been its marking years, chaptering the lives of those who endured them, who went into them from one life-style and with one set of expectations and emerged into a world changed for them out of all recognition.

There are fewer and fewer now who have memories of the First War, but such recollections are sharp, tender, brave and full of pain. Those who have them, seem to look back with awe, marvelling that they lived through such a holocaust and sometimes even smiled.

First though, there is a single, second-hand memory of a much older war, that Millicent Davis has carried with her over all the conflicts of her own lifetime.

> My father was born in the 1870s and he used to tell us that as a small boy he had been taught to do the proper military salute by a retired soldier who'd been young at Waterloo.

Earlier wars than that of 1914 were fought by officer-younger-sons and the 'rough soldiery', and scarcely touched the lives of ordinary men and women. So the echoes of romance and adventure that went with the tale of her father's salute perhaps gave a deceptive thrill to the young Millicent when she heard her father say in the early days of 1914, that he was sure there was going to be a war. But reality was a dark shadow in the wings, and war was scarely declared before young men, who should have been tradesmen, clerks and students, were off to the strange dance of death . . . a brutish life they had never dreamed of leading.

> We were on a painting holiday in Dunning in August 1914 and whenever we came home Herbert, my older brother, joined up . . .

couldn't wait. I've still got his sketch of Dunning Square from that holiday. He went to the Cameron Highlanders.

For all the rumours and certainties that war was coming, the country was caught unawares.

Some of them had no uniforms at first. Britain didn't seem to be prepared. A lot of them just drilled with sticks. I remember seeing that.

It was worth a chuckle in the Second War that the Home Guard was armed with wooden poles, but those men of the First were soldiers no more than a month from the trenches.

Life at home became grey with restriction and shortage and gloomy folk complained at first, but gradually common gumption and imagination, and the shameful realisation of what was happening in France spurred civilians into action. For the playing with poles had soon turned into this bloodiest of wars and stupefying casualty lists began to appear in daily newspapers. Those who had waved off their lads with jingoistic cheering, glorying in their handsome courage, were sobered now and threw themselves into making the best of trifling difficulties at home. As apprentice by apprentice, office boy by office boy, the young disappeared to France, or to sea, older men doubled their workloads by day, and by night rolled up their sleeves to other tasks.

I remember a rough area near us you'd've thought was good for nothing, but it was marked off into allotments for growing vegetables. A lot of business men came off the train with their high bowlers and brollies, got home and changed, and away down to dig and weed their wee patches and try to grow bigger turnips than anyone else.

Older women made small thrifts, boasting of what would have shamed them before. Janet Kay remembers her mother.

She used to cut bits out of the tail of my father's shirt to make new collars and cuffs . . . got quite expert at that.

Younger women hitched up their skirt hemlines to a more practical level, to pour into factories . . . and some found unexpected perks there to help eke out wartime household furbishings. Agnes Grove's mother worked at Templeton's carpet factory.

> They used to make chenille for carpets and if there was a wee bit mistake you could get the strips cheap. My mother would get maybe four and make curtains wi' that . . . for next-to-nothing.

That bargain was too good to be longlasting and those who found it first were the lucky ones.

> When the bosses discovered a woman could *do* things with the likes of these strips they started to charge more.

The chenille-making gradually wound down and eventually stopped altogether for the duration of the war. Looms that had proudly woven carpet for the White House Oval Office went over to more mundane warps and woofs.

> Y'see the looms got put to making army blankets instead, until after the war when they went back to the chenille again.

Lack of chenille and other fancies were the least of the shortages, and basic household supplies were at first scarce and then rationed.

> We went to stay with friends at a farm in Auchterarder during the war, and they gave us . . . *butter!* We hardly ever had butter at home because the small ration you could get wasn't very nice . . . wasn't worth buying. We were better with marg really. There was a kind of art about the way you used your wee lump of ration when you did take it. You all had different ways of eating it. My sister ate all hers on the first slice of bread. I eked it out all through the meal, and my brother kept his to have on the last slice. Showed up our personalities really.

For most families there could be a wee glut of at least one of the rationed foods . . . a modest black market or sly offering from under the counter. Bosom friendship with a grocer was suddenly a great asset, or some tit-for-tat arrangement that allowed the exchange of half-a-dozen oranges for a pound of sugar concluded by grave business men with more in their Gladstone bags than insurance or stockbroking documents. Sometimes it was a case of the early bird . . . Lily Joseph's father was one who knew a fat worm when he saw it.

He knew the right people. He used to go to the butcher at six o'clock in the morning and get a wee bit of whatever was going. And he gave them some of what he had. It was a tight community, they helped each other.

Sometimes the extra was legitimate and smiled on by authority. The making of Mrs. Mysie Kyle's family lemonade was rated as essential.

Sugar was rationed of course, but we got an allowance for making the lemonade, we got enough even for the house, so we didn't need to take up our ordinary ration. But we got a wee bit extra butter instead, because some people couldn't afford theirs.

Some who were too prodigal with their tea-sugar early in the week, were resourceful enough to find a substitute by the end.

We put toffee-balls in our tea if we'd no sugar. You could stir it about a bit, then take it out to keep for the next time.

But long before rationing was biting and queues were long, before the chenille-making stopped or the first carrot-fronds poked up on the allotments, it was apparent that the war that was to have been 'over by Christmas' was only just starting and that civilians would have to find a use in the war effort for whatever talents they could dredge up.

In school we were put to knitting for the troops . . . socks, scarves, balaclava helmets and so on, because it was miserable and cold in the trenches. And we'd to buy things and write wee letters to put in the parcels with the woollies. I can remember putting in boracic powder . . . for the soldiers' feet.

At the receiving end of the parcels one nonagenarrian recalls getting candles and matches sent.

You put the flame up and down the pleats of your kilt for to kill the lice. The sight of us in kilts was s'posed to make Jerry feart . . . the 'Ladies from Hell' they called us. But it wasn't very practical, the kilt . . . not in the muddy hell of Flanders.

Some troops who had been cheered by the messages in their parcels made contact with the writers on their leaves.

> There was a Private Turnbull came to see me twice. He got the V.C. later so he was a star and I was the talk of the class because I knew him.

Another star of the '14–18 War who was right at the other end of the command chain from the good private, caused Bunty Angles to commit the only school misdeameanour she can recall. There were visits round the country of certain big-wigs to rally people from despondency and urge their support for the troops when things at the front were going badly and casualty lists were long.

> The only time I plunked the school was to see Earl Haig going along Great Western Road. We went out at lunchtime and saw him passing along in his big car . . . quite quickly . . . but we did get a glimpse of him. Then we didn't bother to go back to school.

The money for the comforts parcels came from selling home-made toffee or soft goods or paper flowers, from fund-raising concerts and flag days.

> Right through the war I collected on flag-days. The first one I remember was for 'gallant little Montenegro'. I don't know what was happening in 'gallant little Montenegro' but I rattled my can all the same. Then there was'poor Belgium' and the Red Cross. There was no half-measures with me. I was out standing at Cessnock subway before breakfast to get workers coming off their shifts.

'Poor Belgium' had much need of the rattled can for the refugees pouring across its borders after the German invasion, and of the services put at their disposal on their arrival in Scotland. Miss Jenny Logan remembers the quota of them that came to Glasgow, terrified that they'd find it savage and primitive and not a lot better than staying at home under harsh occupation might have been. A warm welcome at Central Station with hot food and brisk organisation to find them comfortable billets surprised and reassured them.

> Quite a lot were put into the Mansion House at Rouken Glen. Our uncle had a lot to do with the whole arrangement because he was

the City Collector. And his wife had been at school in France, so she was fluent in French and interpreted for them. Later for all that she was presented with a signed photo of the King of the Belgians.

As well as the worthy works of comfort and mercy, with knitting-pins and flag-days and the relief of the refugees, there were other skills to offer. Musicians of varying talent dusted down instruments, gargled their throats and set out to entertain low-spirited civilians or the troops themselves . . . to relieve the boredom of waiting for action or cheer convalescent invalids to whom the high adventure had brought broken bodies and haunted minds. Alan Dale's father was one of those who took their music to wherever there was need and ran their own risks in the doing.

> He was a turn in a touring circus at that time . . . a trapeze artist for a bit . . . and a clown. But he played the saxophone as well. In the First War he went round with a group entertaining the troops . . . went to Ireland and so on. One night they missed the ferry from Belfast, and-here that boat was sunk and people lost on its way across.

There were long days for the convalescent sick and wounded sent home from the front and these little groups of 'Good Companions' tried to lighten the gloom.

> My brother was in a wartime hospital in Edinburgh at one stage, ill with trench fever. We were all quite a musical family, and we went as a group to this school in Edinburgh that was the hospital. We entertained the troops there non-stop for a whole day in the main hall. I would be about fourteen. I remember handing out programmes my father had done in his nice script. I sang too. I sang 'The Green Trees Whispered Sweet and Low', and then pantomime songs. My mother and my brother, Harold, played some of my father's musical arrangements. He'd studied music at Leipzig and taught us all.

That was one of the last happy events for the family. Having survived spells of trench fighting throughout the war, since the instant enlisting in August 1914 when he was just eighteen, and come through the dread trench fever, Herbert was killed three weeks before the armistice.

For that was the reality of the war . . . not the sturdy support going on at home, however useful, but the blood-soaked glaur of trench warfare, and the slaughter of a generation there, or in the icy bleakness of winter at sea. And young men could be lost in other ways than by death.

My brother took a kind of depression at the front . . . sort of shell-shock. He'd been the kind and affectionate one of all my brothers, clever too, and humorous. Very steady. But he just stopped writing home altogether . . . lost touch. He got through the last months like a kind of zombie, then when it was over he just went wandering and it was a long time before he eventually came home. Never made anything of life after that. It broke my mother's heart.

And one who didn't come home to the Rodger family at all . . .

. . . my brother was at sea. He jumped ship and had the Navy police after him, so he just disappeared altogether.

There were other old friends who were casualties of war too. Mysie Kyle's family lost their horse to army service.

Big Prince used to draw the lemonade lorry and was stabled at home so he was a great favourite. Well, my father was up at Saracen Street with him one day and these men just came up and said, 'We need your horse' and without a by-your-leave or anything they just led him out the trams and took him away . . . to the war. My father'd to come back home that day for the old horse, Donald, to take him up to Saracen Street and put him in the trams instead. We never saw Prince again. He was killed in France. I was young in the First War, six when it started. There was Prince, and then my uncle was wounded and missing, so I was frightened of the Germans.

There were other horses than Prince called from the pleasant plod of peacetime to the screaming shells of France. Hard times for dobbins. But one not very gruntled Tommy in France saw the conscripted horses as having more comfort and consideration than himself and his mates. Trucks were lined up to take animals and men to the front and large notices posted in French by the allied soldiers making the behind-the-lines arrangements. The Tommies made for the trucks, each vehicle allocated to thirty men, passing the ones to which only five horses were headed. 'Och here,' remarked the private climbing into his cramped quarters, 'I wish't I was a chevvocks and no' a hom' . . . and the old soldier remembers and chuckles.

Mrs. Agnes Grove's husband too saw life at the front with the horses.

He was a lead horse-driver with a six-horse vehicle taking ammunition to the front. Sometimes when he arrived they'd cheer him because they were right out of ammunition. One time the Germans were firing and he got wounded . . . lost part of his leg with shrapnel . . . affected him on that side all his life after.

Having lost Prince, and seen tears for the missing uncle, young Mysie had more trauma to bear.

My brother was taken to the army after that, near the end of the war, and he took yon terrible 'flu that killed so many people. He developed T.B. and was in a sanitorium in the Ochil Hills for a long time.

Bert Paterson was another who left the front with a shattered leg that still troubles him sorely at ninety-two.

I mind how the nurses looked when I came wounded out the trenches . . . looked like angels, in white dresses and white pinnies and caps . . . and crisp kind of cuffs up to their elbows. I can still see that picture after seventy year. And mind a lot of them girls had been lady kind of lassies that couldnae move for their hobble skirts a few years afore. My leg still plays up but I was one of the lucky ones 't got back at all.

Nine million young men on both sides were not so fortunate . . . ten times the entire population of the city of Glasgow were killed in the 1914–18 War . . . every death an individual tragedy.

My younger brother was about eighteen and on embarkation leave when word came that my older brother had been killed. It came in an orange envelope from the War Office. I remember Mamma taking in the telegram and my father taking it from her to open. Oh, the tears of that day! I adored that brother. He was only twenty-two.

The elderly voice, remembering, has no detachment in it that this was over seventy years, another war and long years of marriage ago.

Three weeks after that death came the cease-fire, and for some it was bunnets in the air and dancing in the streets. Agnes Grove was in the streets.

Do I remember the Armistice? oh aye . . . easy! I was working in Templeton's. We all just stopped our looms and got ready to walk out. The tenter says, 'Here, you cannae d'that till we've seen the boss'. The Boss said 'yes' but we'd've been away anyway . . . into the town, all shouting and singing. What a carry-on! Then we got an extra five shillings in our pay that week.

Janet Kay was a little younger, but her recollections of the day, the scenes of relief, and rejoicing, and the players, are just as vivid.

I was in Miss Cay's class at the school (the others used to say she was my granny because of the name). She'd maybe be about thirty-two or three then. She was lovely. I can remember she wore nice coat-frocks. She was like that the day of the Armistice. Well anyway the jannie chapped on the door with the big brass handles (the last jannie had got killed in the war). 'Miss Cay' says this new one, 'can I speak to you?' She went out, and came back into the room, crying. She says 'It's peace'. We'd all to go out to the gallery above the hall that was down below in the dunny, (where you usually marched-in to someone thumping out 'The Flowers of Edinburgh' or that, on an old piano). The headmaster talked to us, we sang 'O God of Bethel' and repeated the Lord's Prayer. I've always had a lump in my throat singing that, since then. Then we got sent home.

For some, the day of the Armistice was not much different from any other and work went doggedly on . . . but it's a day remembered for all that. Robert Ford was still in Portpatrick.

I was labouring on the land at the time the war ended. We could hear the church bells ringing that day, three miles away, but we were in the field gathering up potatoes, and we just went on digging.

That November day held one of Struan Yule's early memories . . .

. . . of seeing a woman across the street struggling to put out a big flag from her window . . . almost falling out. I remember asking my mother what she was doing. And-here it was the end of the war . . . the Armistice.

Peggy Carson danced in an arm-linked trio across Jamaica Bridge, Millicent Davis went from terminus to terminus through the town on the open top of a yellow tram, to see the revellers. Jack Roche went into church. But for many others, it was a day of tears and sorrow.

> My mother and her family weren't throwing their hats in the air. They'd lost their brother and there wasn't much to rejoice about. They were very subdued. My father'd been killed on the Somme and when the Armistice came, my mother just went into the Room with her lips all tight, and shut the door. I was about ten and I didn't know what to say to her. I still had a black ribbon in my dress.

As the surviving men came home and people shook themselves down into routines of living again after the war, the pattern of its results began to show more clearly.

> Almost all the boys in my age-group were lost. It was like nearly a whole generation gone . . . killed in the trenches or drowned. And that left almost a whole generation of women with no chance of marriage. All those good lives wasted . . . and no children to follow them.

Isobel Horn's family was evidence of that.

> My mother was the only one of five sisters to marry. So there was I, living beside a whole household of quite young spinster aunts.

Local War Memorial lists revealed another appalling result of the war and the system of forming comrade-squads from the same places, towns and shires. Robert Ford speaks for his neighbourhood.

> Just about all the boys from our village died, in actions where they were alongside each other. There's about a hundred names on the memorial. Later they put men into regiments and other services, more kind of at random, so they wouldn't be fighting together and all get wiped out.

In the later aftermath, Glasgow, like other places, was too busy licking its own wounds to notice that over in Germany insidious problems were sowing the dragons' teeth of war for the children whom that culled First War generation *had* been able to produce.

One of our professors at the university told us about being in Germany in the inflation period . . . when people were trundling handcarts of money to pay their bills, or suitcases of it to do their shopping.

Jack Roche saw it all in hindsight.

The Armistice of 1918 was just the first half over, of one big-big war. It was just, what you would say? . . . a kind of deadly interval.

13
Epifania was our Big Thing

Festivals are, by their very nature, occasions that don't change much and are for the most part still celebrated . . . if not always with the same awestruck understanding and belief, at least with delight in the secular trimmings and social round. Take Christmas. There's a kind of rosy glow over memories of what they were like in young days when everything was new, exciting and full of promise. There is no talk though of expensive toys or of the expectation that wants would be automatically met.

> I always wanted a bicycle, but I never got that . . . got old ones that other people had done with, but never a shiny new one of my own. And football boots . . . I never got them either. I wanted them badly, but it was always just someone's old ones that were always too big or too small and gave you blisters . . . or they'd maybe a nail in them. So I couldn't play proper school footb'll . . . just in the street or a bare patch of grass beside the burn. But I did get one thing I wanted. I got a Meccano set one Christmas . . . the basic set that my uncles added to for me.

Little Mary Rodger got cinders in her stocking for luck. Just how lucky was she in her finds as she delved past the clinkers?

> No' a right stocking . . . more a wee sort of bag . . . with an apple a wee poke of sweeties and the cinders. But the best was the tuppence you got at the bottom . . . you fairly scattered the rest to get at that.

No Barbie dolls, computers or high-tech everything for the likes of the McLean Street Rodgers. Bunty Angles fared rather better at her grandmother's home.

> Oh I always got a stocking. They filled it with a tangerine, an apple, some sweeties and chocolate and a sixpence. And I remember once,

because it was my favourite tea, my uncle, for fun, putting some ham and an egg in my stocking.

. . . hopefully hard-boiled!

And I always got a small present as well.

Mysie Kyle's memories are more of the season's socialising than its loot.

We went down to Blochairn Church for the service and for the Christmas Eve 'swarry' in the big hall. You got a bag of buns and a cup of tea. Then New Year's Day it was the Sunday School prize-giving. You got your prize, and an orange going out at the door.

Eighty years ago Christmas was certainly not the extravagant thrash it is now, nor even the most widely celebrated day in the Christian calendar, and many Reformed Kirk folk looking back, recall more excitement at New Year, which held none of the dubious hang-overs from midwinter pagan festivals.

We didnae do much at Christmas forbye we got wee bits of presents and stockings. There was no work holiday for your father and we never-ever had a tree or that.

But New Year . . . ah New Year was different!

Come Ne'erday my mother went daft. It was a room and kitchen and ever'thing got cleaned for dear life, brasses polished, curtains washed, range cleaned (never mind it was scoured and blackleaded every week anyway) the flues were done . . . even the ceiling got white-washed . . . kitchen table scrubbed (again!). You'd of thought black shame on yoursel's if you went dirty into the New Year. It was all ready the night before really . . . for Hogmanay.

There must have been Edwardian women who slittered cloths over kitchen tables from time to time, who let their brasses turn dingy or left rims of grease round their jaw-boxes, but none of them were the mothers of any of the loyal offspring who remembered for these pages.

Mamma scoured every corner for Hogmanay and put clean sheets and poinds on the beds, to go spotless into the New Year. The table would be set too because your first visitors would arrive at midnight. Us young ones would be in nightdresses or pyjamas, but you got to taste the shortbread or blackbun and the ginger wine . . . Crabbe's . . . no' very nice really, but you sat there mim as a pussy cat and sipped it. Most of the visiting was done the next day, you *had* callers and you *went* visiting . . . in your Sunday braws. You took ginger wine with you or a wedge of your own black bun.

In some homes there was the annual skiddle of brewing their own wine.

It was my Da made the ginger in our house . . . got a wee bottle of essence and brown sugar, fairly fancied himself at that job. It wasnae the ginger he fancied *himself* though.

Italian winter solstice celebrations were even later than 1st January, as Mr. Mario Servadei remembers.

Italian families when I was young didn't hold Christmas as such . . . not very much. Not on 25th December. And New Year wasn't anything special either. We looked more to what we called Epifania on 6th January.

Epifania (Epiphany) celebrated the visit of the Wise men to the stable with their gifts.

Epifania was our big thing when the immigrants came here at first. Now of course Italians have taken up with the Scottish ways . . . did that quite early on. I remember that because my father always had to first foot the people up the stair.

Later in the year, Easter celebrations were a poor shadow of what they had been in the homeland.

It's always an important festival in the church in Italy but when the Italians came here they lost the Easter procession and all the Saints' days processions too. Maybe if the Italians hadn't scattered all through Britain when they came, but kept together in a 'quarter' like the ones that emigrated to New York they'd have kept up the old customs the way they do there.

And Mario Servadei senses another difference in the fates of immigrants to the two countries.

Then they became American almost at once. Maybe because America was a hotch-potch of nationalities already, trying to weld themselves together into one; while here, Italians were foreigners among the British. When my cousin over there talks of 'my country' he means America. When I talk about 'my country' I mean Italy . . . though maybe I would call myself Scots-Italian.

Before there ever were great Christian festivals to celebrate, Jewish people were holding the selfsame feasts and rituals they enjoy today . . . highlighting the turning seasons with gatherings and rejoicings hallowed since the days of Abraham. They seem perhaps less splendid now than they did when Lily Balarsky was a child.

Chanukah was always a great festival with us. It's all about the story of the oil in the Temple lasting for eight days . . . a miracle . . . the Miracle of Lights. I remember the Chanukah candles burning brightly and vividly when I was small. The family takes it in turn that week to light the candles. I was one of the young ones so I'd to wait until late in the week. When I was very wee my father guided my hand. Then the fifth night we got what Jews call 'Chanukah gelt' . . . wee presents of money your parents and friends gave you. There were parties too with latkas and doughnuts and songs . . . 'Moaz Tsur' and a Yiddish song telling the Chanukah tale, 'Little lights, you have stories to tell'. It's still a great festival, but oh! I loved it when it was all new and magic to me.

Apart from comparatively recently relaxing into festivity at Christmas time, and marking Easter by the rolling of eggs to celebrate the rolling away of Christ's tombstone, the Presbyterian and other reformed Kirks in Scotland have never been greatly 'into' festivals. Their people can only envy the pleasure and hospitality of the Muslims at Eid-ul-Fitr after the fasting month, the Hindus' Diwali and the long and hearty Chinese New Year . . . and the all-through-the-year celebrations punctuating Jewish life.

In the spring of the Jewish calendar year comes the ancient Feast of the Passover.

We didn't go much to parties but we did a lot of visiting among our own people, all together in the community around Saltmarket, the

Briggait and the Gorbals. Passover was a big thing in our family . . .
with as many as you could seat, no matter the size of the house. Then
when everyone was gathered my father would tell the story of the
Passover from the Haggada. In those days the preparations weren't
all commercialised the way they are now. There wasn't the money.
But, mind you, maybe we'd more the spirit of it all. Like you do
at Christmas, I suppose, you lose a wee bit of what it's really all
about, under all the trimmings. There's wee practical things too,
about modern life . . . your expensive carpet gets awful messed up
with unleavened bread . . . it was easier in the old days to sweep the
crumbs off the lino.

Ah, who was it said with feeling. 'They're weel-aff that's no' weel-
aff'. Even weekly Friday night Shabbos celebrations (touched on
in another chapter) are not quite what they were in days when
entertainment was not so suffocatingly available at the touch of a
button.

Jewish Friday nights used to be so special . . . much more sacred than
now. Your mother had had a hard week, washing and cleaning and
often helping in some wee family business. But on a Friday night
she sat down with us all. It was nice that, in the candle-light . . . all
the polishing and cleaning done on the Thursday. I still have the old
candlesticks that came with my mother from Lithuania.

The big day for the Jewish male is neither weekly nor annual.
It is, as it always has been, the once-in-a-life-time, ever to be
remembered day of his Bar Mitzvah, celebrated at puberty. Here
too, there's the shaking of an older head over the altered emphasis
on the customs surrounding it.

When I was young Bar Mitzvahs were quite simple . . . very serious
but simple . . . the most important occasion in a boy's life. My
husband Solomon Balarsky is over eighty now and when he had his
he went to the synagogue in the Gorbals, read his piece and his father
gave him *a whole sixpence*, and he thought that was a very good gift.
Just the same as now he'd to learn the Hebrew rhythm and chanting
of the Torah (that's part of the Pentateuch . . . first five books of the
Bible). It was the most important part of the Bar Mitzvah, still is, but
there's a lot of expensive presents now that maybe a boy thinks about
more than the meaning of the whole thing.

Not all ritual observances were conventionally religious. Mrs. Lily Joseph recalls her father's pride in his weekly occasion.

> He became a mason, got initiated in 1902 at Bath Street. Only one of all my brothers did it later, they were the only ones in the whole family. Oh, my father was like Beau Brummel when he went to his meeting . . . all dressed up. He'd a best suit made to measure specially. Th'were lots of tailors near where we lived in the Gorbals. And he'd this private drawer where he kept all his Masonic accoutrements. These things were very very secret and nob'dy else got to open that drawer.

Drama, theatre and the good life woven together. That was what Masonic secrets looked like to the uninitiated.

It's small wonder Glaswegians of past times whooped it up at New Year or saved up hard for the July Fair on Glasgow Green (or if they were bien and very lucky, for a trip down the Clyde) for they had precious few of the structured and ancient ceremonies that immigrant minorities enjoyed and still keep now. There were commemorations though, very stiff and British . . . very worthy, but recalled in elderly days with pleasure. Janet Kay was an ardent member of the Red Cross.

> It was a big event every year on the Sunday nearest to Florence Nightingale's birthday (this would be about twenty years or less after her death) we'd this big-big assembly of nurses, hundreds and hundreds parading to Glasgow Cathedral. I remember once, and the place packed with nurses, the organ broke down and we'd to sing to a wee piano in yon great big building . . . couldnae hear it at all. But the good thing was . . . just *being* there.

Red Cross marches seem kind of tame beside Eid-ul-Fitr and Chanukah, but the Calvinists among us acknowledge that the old Kirk didn't leave us much of a legacy of merrymaking festivals and that we have to content ourselves with having pulled Christmas back out of the gloom to rejoice over its essential meaning, smothering our Yuletide trees with tinsel, and our friends with Magi gifts.

14
A Nice Pannyma

Funny i'nt it, how you take a wee case and go and stay in someb'dy else's house. I wonder who ever thought holidays up.

In ancient days from season to season kings moved about their realms from one residence to another so that they could collect taxes and so that their subjects in each area took it in turns to supply the court with goods and services during the time it was held on their doorsteps. The Prince Regent's time was long after that, so maybe he was really the one who, with his sea dips at Brighton, began the whole idea of holidays. Queen Victoria was partial to them of course, and the layers of folk up there beside her had, for decades past, changed houses for 'the season'. But it was when a web of railway lines and 'bus services was spun across the country that the notion percolated down to the plebs and they began to explore the possibilities of transplanting their families to live for a week or two away from their natural city habitat.

'Transplant' was certainly the word for the operation, whatever the destination, be it seaside, country, or in rare cases, overseas. The whole project had to be planned like a military operation. There was no lifting the boot of the car, throwing in a case filled with easy-care fabrics and casual jeans . . . and setting off in tops and trainers, and hatless (unless for a kiss-me-quick or Spanish sombrero).

Oh no. It was a serious matter was the annual holiday. Take the Clyde coast brigade and the Lockie family's drill.

My first recollection of holidays would be about 1905 and going to Lochranza. I enjoyed myself when I got there, but my best memories

are of getting ready to go, and the cabby coming to collect you for
your month away. You'd to take everything, all your linen . . .
for beds, table and towels, cutlery too . . . and the cat, always the
cat . . . the whole jing-bang. We'd a big Saratoga trunk with a
convex lid, a compartment for hats and a long place for umbrellas
and parasols. As well's that, you'd your hat-box and the hamper
of clothes that you closed up with a rod that went through two
loops.

That was the flitting ready and the family assembled in gloves, hats
and best coats, waiting for the cart. When the man came he heaved
the luggage first on to his back and then up to the front of the cab.
Then there was one last ritual before the big 'Gee-up!'

I'd always a wee bag with loaf sugar in it to give to the horse . . . held
it out on the palm of my hand the way my father showed me.

Then it was up and into the cab.

Now whenever I smell leather . . . I'm right back in that cab. Smells
take you back, don't they? (you don't get it with plastic though).
Anyway then we were off clip-clopping to the Broomielaw for the
boat. Did that for years.

The getting-there was much the same for the Logan family except
that they were setting off for the train, but dressed again in the good
Sunday braws for the travelling. At the end of the train journey a
waggon met them at the station to take them the five or six miles
to the rooms where 'attendance' awaited them . . . for a month.

The hamper was lifted up to the front beside the driver and we sat down,
two at each side at the back, the wee ones up on knees.

After a lifetime since these days, Miss Mabel and Miss Jenny Logan
can list their holiday places over the years without faltering . . .
Oban, Drummore, Cairnryan, then Elie and Port Logan and the
rest.

Or if it was Skipness, the horse and trap came to the pier instead of the
station, to take us to the holiday house. We'd always a long holiday,
because our father was a teacher.

Lily Balarsky's family, after the settling-in years as immigrants,
was established enough to have their holiday from the close in

Stockwell Street . . . a trip 'doon the watter' was skittles compared
to the rigours of the journey from Lithuania and certainly didn't
daunt her parents. Even so, it was a more complicated expedition
than for Gentile families.

> It was always the Clyde coast. We took a room or two and did for
> ourselves . . . we couldn't have taken rooms-with-attendance, because
> of our food laws. So it was a big thing taking all your dishes and utensils,
> we wouldn't have used other peoples . . . that's just our way of life. The
> food was different from theirs too because the van would come from
> Glasgow to the Jewish holiday-makers down the Clyde with our kind
> of meat and bread. *We* had great holidays . . . but not the mothers. It
> was hard for them.

With Janet Kay it was Rothesay.

> Oh yes, Ro'say . . . a fortnight in May. I got off school for being a wee
> bit delicate. I was top of the class too, . . . a right wee genius. In the
> Elementary anyway. (It was a different matter in the Secondary!). But
> whatever it was, I got off the school to go to Ro'say in May. We went
> Third Class to Wemyss bay and then 'Cabin' to Bute. Just my mother
> and me; my father came at weekends. When I was very wee he didn't
> get paid holidays at Singers where he worked, and I'll never forget the
> day my mother told me 'Your father's got put on the *staff*' . . .

as distinct from the practical work force. . .

> . . .so now he'll get two weeks *paid* holidays.

'Rooms-with-attendance' was certainly the preferred way to take
your holiday. It was a cut above just taking a room. You'd still your
accommodation and brought in your own food, but the landlady
cooked it for you. Part of the gamble was whether or not your
hostess 'spoiled good butcher meat' or 'washed the lettuce right'.
Another that she might be a dark presence keeping a baleful eye on
her premises. All the same, rooms-with-attendance was the thing
for most families, until at least the thirties.

When holiday-makers and hampers were reunited and mother
had spent a tantalisingly slow hour or more, unpacking, with the
young hopping from one foot to the other waiting for the sandshoes
or the bathing-costume to appear, the holiday was 'on'.

My big sister had a striped bathing dress that I envied. I always wish't I looked like our Lizzie. When I look back on thon costume it was loose, no waist, hung from shoulders that buttoned together the front to the back. And it was long. But it was above her knees and that was s'posed to be daring. My Ma and Pa argy-bargy'd about that. But what I liked was it had her initials on the chest! Oh, Lizzie was something! And here's me in just my baggy cotton costume. Och, but I wish't I was Lizzie.

It might be that what came out of the trunk first, was the beach dress as opposed to *un*dress.

Me and my sister would be at the Punching Judy (sic) or playing buckets and spades on the sand and we'd have on long cotton pinafores and big straw hats (I'm talking around 1910). My father had a blue suit and a yellow panama hat, and I can see my mother yet in a deck chair wearing a great big hat with flowers and quite a heavy coat in what she'd've called 'covert' coating.

Janet Kay had one holiday outfit that remained indelibly stamped on her embarrassed mind.

We went to the entertainers, and-here it was Charlie Kemble this night. He used to pick out people in the audience and make up songs about them as he went along. Well he pointed at me and began to sing that I was . . .
   'Sitting pretty
   With my Daddy and my Mammy
   With a wee red coat and a wee white tammy.
Well! I was absolutely mortified . . . didn't know where to put myself . . . just wanted to cry. But my mother nudged me quite chuffed. 'Listen, it's you he's singing about. It's great.' But I didn't think it was great. *I was insulted.* There was the Palace pictures too, at Ro'say. I was never allowed to go to the Saturday matinées anywhere else. It s'posed to be rough . . . and I was delicate and precious.

Another who was mortified at certain holiday visions was Peggy Carson.

My father insisted on wearing his shirt and braces *and* a knotted handkerchief on his head. He was a bald a bit and the hankie was to keep it from burning. I hated that. Thought it looked silly. 'Never heed, Hen,' I mind him sayin', 'you wouldnae want your Da to get

sunstroke'. Other men wore what my mother called 'a nice pannyma'. Come to think on it, hats were quite a thing wi' my parents. My father used to begin all his stories about his young days, 'When I was a lad in a doo-lander . . .'

Some destinations depended on strategically placed grannies or other kin. And sometimes without them there would have been no holiday at all. Ann Hutchison and her family relied on their auntie at Irvine.

> She'd her own house so we didn't go with a big hamper. Anyway we hadnae that much to put in a big hamper. She'd a beautiful garden with apple trees, so we played there and we paddled down at the shore.

Another granny had a house at Millport, and her daughter at least, among all the remembered mothers, was not slavishly thirled to the change of sink.

> We went there a lot, whole family loved the sea. My mother once sailed with her father and brother in a sailing-boat from Gourock round the Cock of Arran.

It was boats with Richard Fram too . . . and a built-in grandfather at Dunoon. He spent hours watching the procession of steamers that plied the Clyde.

> . . . used to see the yellow and black steamer funnels on the boats from Gourock . . . and the red and blue from Glasgow, and I think red, blue and white from Craigendoran. When the steamers came in they would disgorge their passengers and there would be horse-drawn carriages for the posh people, and then a bit lower down the scale men with handcarts to take hampers and trunks to the boarding-houses. And there would be wee boys . . . 'Can I carry your bag Mister?'

That service wasn't too popular with everyone, as Jack Roche recalls.

> The right porters didnae like that mind . . . losin' their trade to the wee boys; because the porters was licen'd and had their badges.

Richard Fram enjoyed the puffers too. They were the sturdy little work-horses of the river, supplying the small holiday towns beading the shores of the Firth.

As well as the steamer pier at Dunoon there was a wee stone one, called the 'coal' pier. It was for the puffers that came in every day with their loads of coal and building material. Great wee boats with just a skipper and mate and maybe an engineer (like in Para Handy). The puffers got unloaded by a big arm with a bucket that would swing over a cart on the wee quay. They were called puffers because they worked like railway engines and the smoke came out in puffs. The islands further north depended on them for sugar and paraffin and all that sort of thing.

Young Richard's grandfather had a few other pleasures up his sleeve to share with his visitor, forbye pointing out funnels and puffs of smoke.

He'd built a twelve-foot rowing boat that he told me he'd made for £1 per foot of length. Cost him £16 altogether with the rowlocks and foot spars. Sounds cheap but that would be several weeks' wages for a working man then. And he made a spear-fishing box one summer with a glass panel to see through at the stern. I would hang over with my spear made out of a broom handle and a toasting fork. We caught flounders like that and we never came home without a 'fry'. Oh, I liked Dunoon.

Small wonder with so ingenious a grandfather at hand. Mrs. Millicent Davis was fascinated, if not by all the craft that rocked or plunged on the Clyde, at least by certain particular ones. Her father was a design engineer at Fairfields.'

When we were very small and on holiday at Kilcreggan, *The Empress of Canada* was on her trials. We put up an old tablecloth to fly like a flag when she went past, and they used to give us a peep on the *Empress's* hooter as they came level . . . I think my father must've put them up to it.

Some day, in their turn, the young of present-day back-pack-safaris to India, Africa and Bangkok and their exotic explorations of little-known corners of Europe, will look back too. But however exciting their recollections as they sit in the Eventide homes of the 2050s, those memories will lack the common strands that bind todays octogenarians, with their shared memories of going down the Clyde. Of all the rememberers for these pages, only one had never holidayed there . . . Rothesay, Dunoon, Helensburgh,

Innellan, Troon, Prestwick, Ayr, Kilcreggan, Strone, Tighna-
bruaich, and a dozen other villages each had its devotees, seeing
them still in sharp bright pictures, and knowing smells and
sensations even now, that have remained with them for a lifetime.

> When I close my eyes I can still feel the sting of salt water, and the
> rubbing down wi' a rough towel my Ma had special for the bathing.

> With me it was the Arran chip-van that come round at night, and
> you went out for your poke of chips. And there was Woolley's shop
> at Brodick that I couldn't understand when I was wee. 'Woolies' to
> me should've had big gold letters on red, and sold everything at
> Thruppence and Sixpence.

But recollections, however sharp they seem in memory, can trick
us in our westering years . . .

> I remember above the pier at Dunoon was a statue of Flora Macdonald,
> y'know, the one that helped Bonnie Prince Charlie to escape after
> Culloden. Well, this statue was known locally as Highland Mary, I
> don't know why.

Ah well, perhaps good rememberer, that was because the statue *is*
of Highland Mary, the Argyll lass who loved Robert Burns too
well. A fine woman Flora Macdonald, but not monumented at
Dunoon!

Even those loyal to the Costa Clyde though, spread their wings
from time to time and tasted the delights of other parts.

> Sometimes we went to St. Monance in Fife for a change, wi' its red tiles
> and crowsteps and the big model fishing boat that hung in the kirk.
> Nearly every family in the village had to do wi' the fishing. And you
> used to hear the Salvation Army band in the streets wi' their instruments
> and their streaming ribbons. It was 'dry' then, was St. Monance, and the
> men used to complain and take the 'bus to Anstruther on a Friday night
> to get what they called 'a wee bit petrol for wir engines'.

But it seems ironical that it was those who had been of struggling
immigrant stock who had the more far-travelled and adventurous
holidays. Eileen Reilly, for one, went further than St. Monance.

> I used to be left for the summer at a house in Magherafelt in Ireland
> that had belonged to my great-grandmother. By my time it was her

daughter, my grandmother's sister, that was there. Quite a character she was. She'd worked as a cook in a big house in America, then developed arthritis . . . quite crippled she was . . . and had to come home to Ireland. She walked with crutches so she'd closed off the top storey of her cottage . . . just lived downstairs. So there she was, after the big glitzy, mod-con houses in America, back to the turf fire, oil lamps and the open grate with a swee to cook at. She'd a dog and hens and sometimes if she'd a wee weakly chick that was 'awfie no' weel', she'd a box at the fire to nurse it in, wrapped round in woolly things till it recovered. And, crutches and all, and old-old really . . . she was great with the turf fire.

Not just with the likes of soups and stews but fancies as well.

She used to make a lemon meringue pie. She'd rake the glowing peats apart and lower her big black pot down into it, with the lemon pie inside, as if it was an oven. Then she put the lid on and piled the red-hot turf all round it and over the lid. Can you imagine what it was like to a city child to see this delicious thing coming out of that kind of pot-oven?

The old lady had a way, too, with other children than her own Glasgow visitor.

She was marvellous. All the Catholic and Protestant children that didn't mix much elsewhere came to her house to play with me . . . didn't matter what they were.

Young Eileen with her summer playmates learned early the origin of the milk that just *arrived* on the cart at home in Glasgow . . . and of real water that didn't simply trickle from a tap into the tenement kitchen jaw-box.

I went to a neighbour's farm with a long-handled can every morning for the fresh milk. And there was no running water at the cottage, so I got to fill buckets from a spring-well beside the house.

There were Magherafelt picnics and berry-gathering excursions with pony and trap . . . raspberries and brambles.

That was with the Cuddons. They were a great big family and they'd a hedge I always remember. It was all topiary work, and one of the things was an old man sitting in a chair smoking his pipe . . . all hedge! I thought it was marvellous.

There was a gauntlet to be run though, before she reached the Cuddons'.

> The thing they had that I didn't like was the geese they kept near the front door, that kept running at your legs. I was frightened of them. But oh, I loved those cottage holidays.

And then it was back from paradise to Duke Street.

Another who recalls more distant holidays, to keep in touch with family roots, was Mario Servadei.

> I'd still grandparents in Italy in the thirties, and I remember two holidays there when I was young. But that was a big thing. Travelling abroad wasn't ordinary like it is now. Families like ours had to save for about twenty years to get back to see their folks in Italy. One of the times I stayed there when I was a wee boy was for several months, so I got to know my grandparents quite well. It was a very simple wee country village and that was different for me from the likes of Glasgow.

Not every remembered break, wherever it was, was a two-or-more week idyll of uninterrupted bliss, certainly not in the unchancy days of the First War. Mrs. Mysie Kyle recalls a blighted holiday in 1918.

> We always used to go on holiday with my granny. She was very strict my granny, nippy y'know. We went with her because my mother couldn't get away. The last time was in 1918 at Bridge of Weir. My auntie was with us that year and while we were away she heard that her husband had got wounded and was missing at the front. We came home. We couldn't do anything about it. But everybody just wanted home.

Some holidays were short, not because of bad news, but because funds themselves were short.

> We just always had a coupla days . . . a week-end like . . . out at an old cottage wi' an outside lavvy, at the Mearns. There was this old body . . . she'd a kinda clapped-out face and shuffled about in her baffies . . . well she let out rooms at so-much a night. The cottage is no' there now, and Mearns is just Glasgow. But it was a long way out then.

Shorter even than that tantalising glimpse of the country, was what Lily Joseph's family, still with its fortune to make as immigrants, called a holiday, early in the century. And it's maybe fitting to close the chapter down the Clyde with Mrs. Joseph's memory of the Glasgow Fair.

A holiday? We'd a holiday every year . . . just the Monday . . . Fair Monday. You left early with all your food and there was this public-house in Rothesay Gallowgate, that allowed children and gave you a private room. You could go in there at dinnertime and have your food there. Then th'was the entertainers or just walks and a wee look at the shops. At teatime we'd have a picnic at the Skeoch Woods. It was always sunshine in those days.

15

Clydebank was just Rubble

The 'deadly interval' between the wars that Mr. Jack Roche looked back on in an earlier chapter was over. Scarcely believing it to be possible, people still weary from 1918, and still mourning young men (many of whom would still have been only in their thirties had they lived) came to the autumn of 1939 sliding into conflict yet again. But a lot of things had happened in the intervening years. Aircraft, and methods of flying them, were more sophisticated, and R.A.F. men were fighting this time from home bases, returning night by night from war to home communities, their losses countable from below as they flew back in from sorties. And civilians themselves faced the chance of death from air raid. Radio too was less primitive. The 'wireless' was a fact of life in every living-room, reporting hour by hour on victory or defeat, and the newsreel film a feature in every cinema programme. There was therefore much more overlapping of fighting and home fronts, much more general public involvement, so that memories of this Second War do not belong exclusively to a band of veterans set apart by years of sickening trench warfare that nobody else could begin to comprehend.

This is a book of memories of Glasgow people, not just of city life, and between 1939 and 1945 young Glasgow was abroad in Europe, Africa, South-East Asia, Canada or at British bases far from home. And so the recollections from those years tell how city folk fared in far-flung places during an experience most would have been glad to forego, but which nevertheless in some measure enriched and matured their lives.

In spite of the Royal Navy being the Senior Service, it's 'army, navy and air force' or 'soldiers, sailors and airmen' that is the order of words that rattles most easily off the tongue. So let's start with an army rememberer.

> I'd never been out the country when I joined the army in the first week of September 1939 and between then and 1945 I was in France, wounded a bit at Dunkirk, went to the North African desert, Italy then Germany. I was that glad to get home I thought I would never-ever want to go abroad again.

There's surely evidence that Home Life, not Truth is the first casualty of war, and it was certainly so with the young Balarskys, now thoroughly absorbed in British life.

> My husband was called up to the army and was away abroad for four years. I was at home with a wee son, so he was five before his father came back and we were able to have our daughter. Five years is a long time between children but that was the war for you. My husband was with the Intelligence and worked a lot behind enemy lines and doing de-coding.

Conscripted men came in all shapes and sizes, and lack of soldierly bearing was no indication of potential.

> When we were in the army training camp we'd a wee skinny Glasgow chap . . . wee runty sorta fella. And-here he used to sit on his bunk doing crochet . . . crochet! But when it came time in the fighting, losh me, but he was a demon! Won a Military Medal. I always mind Ernie now when I meet the wee kinda man I used to think a bit Jessie.

But another rememberer was advised in so-many words to stick to the 'Jessie' side of war.

> I was in the Royal Engineers and thought I wanted into a fighting unit. I told the old colonel and he just walked up and down with me and said,
>   'Just you content yourself where you are. I saw men killed all round me in the last war and it wasn't nice.'
>   I must've been daft, I think, to want the fighting. Anyway I stayed where I was.

Another development in this war was the service of the mass of women who offered themselves or were called up. Some who volunteered muddied the waters a little at home in their eagerness

to join up. Mrs. Helen Thomson's mother, for one, did not know
a volunteer from a pressed 'man'.

> I was working in the bank and reserved at first. Then when we were
> de-reserved I joined up and told my mother I was called up. I went to
> Newbattle Abbey for three weeks of showering and de-lousing and so
> on, and a bit of initial training. From there I was sent with two others
> for N.C.O. training.

She puts that selection down to being able to do joined-up
writing and having 'maybe a wee bit initiative'. First it was
one stripe, then three, as a sergeant. But it was her later
commissioned rank of Second Lieutenant that she describes
as . . .

> . . . the lowest of the low. My first posting from officer-training at
> O.C.T.U. was to one of two big houses commandeered for A.T.S.
> girls in Morningside, Edinburgh. I looked after their pay there.

Her mother never did come to grips with what was officially
'what' in military terms and was again duped over her daughter's
next display of patriotic fervour.

> I got the chance to go abroad. I'd two years still to do, but to go abroad
> I'd to sign on for five years So again, I didn't tell my mother that . . .;
> just said I was posted. Anyway I was sent to Cairo as a quarter-mistress
> at a big barracks beside the Nile. The girls in the barracks were mess
> workers, typists and so on. I saw to them, as well as looking after all
> the stocks and the native workers in the kitchens.

On the personal side Cairo was great.

> About ten men to every woman! A lot of the men were invalided back
> there from the desert. And we were well-looked after by servants in
> their jellabas, white loose gowns y'know. And A.T.S. officers were
> automatically made members of the pukka Gazira Club. There was
> tennis and swimming and riding there, and good food.

Less salubrious postings followed, including six months back
home at Moreton-in-Marsh, with merciless weather and even
rebellion to cope with.

> Conditions in the ice and snow with no coal were frightful. The girls
> staged a sit-down strike that I'd to sort out. Didn't blame them really.

It was hardly the Indian Mutiny but it added to the general gloom, and was followed by worse.

> The thaw came. Everything flooded and we'd to move about the camp from Nissen hut to Nissen hut in a small boat. I finished my service days there on that kind of sour note.

An army man with memories of another flooding was Alan Dale.

> Once we'd to pitch our tents on a sea of mud at Taranto in Italy, where there'd just been an outbreak of some plague. Then suddenly, from trying to cope with that, we were sent off with just blankets, rifles and bandoliers of ammunition into Greece. There was fighting there at the end of the war between the Greek forces and the Eoka groups that were trying to get Greece into the Eastern bloc. It was dreadful. People at home didn't realise. There were academics and artists being killed off and there were bodies in the streets as we went about. I was eighteen months in Greece, latterly in Macedonia helping the Greek army to deal with raids from Bulgaria and Yugoslavia taking children away over the border to bring up as communists. It was all very sad. The guerilla troops had been on our side earlier in the war. It was said they'd got financed in those days by the British dropping gold sovereigns into their patches of territory. It was all very confusing and puzzling.

Mr. Hamish Thomson wasn't a bit puzzled fifty-odd years ago, certainly not at the beginning of the war, or even before that. He knew exactly why he chose to volunteer for the R.A.F. early in 1939. He presents himself as something of an anti-hero.

> I knew I would have to go to the war if it came and I fancied the air force. There was the flying of course, but really because if I was going to be killed, I wanted it to be quick. As well as that, I thought it would be more comfortable to go out on raids or fights or whatever, and be back to Britain each night . . . not be slogging it out abroad in trenches with the army.

It was certainly home bases for the first month or two.

> I trained at Prestwick as a Gunner/Wireless Operator, then in Wales on Hawker Hinds, wee bi-planes with open cockpits that you hung out of, y'know. After that it was Fairy Battles and Wellingtons.

But that was the end of home comforts for many a long day.

> One day someone came in . . . 'Anyone here train on Fairy Battles?' I was daft enough to say 'yes', and that was it. Off to France. Dunkirk was still on and the Germans were on their way to Paris. Three of us went to No. 12 Squadron, and we had just five operational flights, dive-bombing bridges and road junctions. Then on the 13th June we were strafing troops and we were hit. We went on fire and crash-landed. The pilot had his hands burned badly. We ran a bit from the plane as it was exploding . . . nowhere to go really. Then two Germans on a motor-bike and side-car came along and, brave men, we just put our hands up . . . 'Come and get us' sort of thing. So the five of us just went off on the bike and side-car. That was that. I hardly saw the war at all.

Maybe not. Nevertheless there were forced marches, hunger, cold and prison camps for long years after that. But these belong with other tales of confinement later in the chapter. Meanwhile we leave young Hamish, scarcely twenty and a prisoner-of-war, and take a glance at Mario Servadei's service days. There were ironic quirks of fate in war when you were of immigrant stock.

> In the First War Italians went into an Italian contingent of the British army. But it was different in the Second War. My father'd been an interpreter doing liaison work between the British and Italian governments during the First War and when the next one came he wasn't interned. But my older brother was taken away as an enemy alien and sent to the Isle of Man. Yet later on I served in the R.A.F. That was war for you. Funny things happened.

Funny things happened in the navy too, or at least little twists of circumstance. Richard Fram's days on his grandfather's rowing-boat, and watching liners come and go on the Clyde, were long past by the time war came.

> The *Empress of Britain* had always been a ship that I remembered and admired. Big liners like that had to anchor at the Tail-of-the Bank and passengers got ferried from there. She was a real beauty.

Then in the war I was a Radio Officer at sea and I had the sad experience of receiving her distress signals when she was attacked by a German raider, and sinking. Couldn't help thinking of the way I'd last seen her at the Tail-of-the-Bank with the sun on her funnels.

Another who went to sea was Jimmy Dewar . . .

I got my call-up papers for the Royal Navy, but I had already been at sea before the War as an apprentice. So I hurried up and joined the Seamen's Union and got taken on the *Arundel Castle* at £6/10s a month. I was away on her with a shipload of troops while the R.N. was still chasing me up. I was with her for quite a long time around the Middle East, Suez and Africa. After that I was on a couple of Atlantic tramps doing convoys. We were in action in 1942 on the *Cape Race* off Iceland. The ship alongside was blown up and we were torpedoed. We thought. We put the two life-boats over and pulled away, and sat out there to watch the *Cape Race* sinking. But she didn't. Nothing happened. She sat there all innocent and empty like the *Marie Celeste*, or what was it . . . 'idle like a painted ship upon a painted sea', because there was a treacly sort of swell all round her. The captain decided the explosion had been from the other ship and that we'd better get back aboard. When we joined the convoy again we just muttered that our problem had been 'bad coal, bad coal'. Didn't want to admit the truth.

There wasn't bad coal or any other kind of smokescreen fibbery needed shortly afterwards when they really *were* followed by a submarine, and torpedoed properly.

. . . into the boats again and this time for about twenty minutes we did watch the *Cape Race* tip up vertically, with all the timber cargo sliding off the deck. Then she sank, bubble, bubble, bubble! We were left to wait until a corvette, *H.M.S. Dianthus*, picked us up. She was already full of U-boat prisoners and Greek survivors from another ship. I found a place beside a funnel and sat there for five days in scarcely any clothes and no shoes, until we got to Liverpool. I got a pair of sandshoes off the Red Cross there and then came home on four weeks 'torpedo' leave.

He had a graphic picture of his next ship.

She'd a wee thin funnel so we called her 'Willie Woodbine'.

Willie Woodbine shifted her cargo and sank not long after the War with the loss of all hands, but by that time Jimmy Dewar, by now an officer, was sailing the oceans in yet another ship, crossing and re-crossing the date line, the Equator and finally the Pacific.

> We'd a broken-down chronometer on that ship and I navigated with an alarm clock that I'd bought at the pawnbroker's in Pollokshaws.

If war changed life dramatically for those who were in the services, there were altered routines on the home front too, and from the outset more profound shifts of civilian activity and energy than in any previous war. Maids departed, and women who had depended on them while they window-shopped in the city or took tea at Miss Cranston's, rolled up their own sleeves and did, not only their own cooking, but marathons of fry-ups in city service canteens as well. Middle-aged men who had dozed over their evening papers or tended their roses, dug up their plots and planted vegetables, and trained as fire-fighters, Home Guards or Air Raid Wardens.

> I can always mind my old navy blue tin hat wi' the W on it, and the stirrup pump and the bucket of sand in the lobby.

Even before the war a number of Glasgow homes had welcomed the sad little trickle of child refugees coming out of Europe. Millicent Davis recalls how richly repaid her family felt later for having opened their hearts to Dorothea from Czechoslovakia.

> Sometime in the thirties there was a movement to bring young Jews out of dangerous situations in Europe . . . looking for offers of homes. There was a man on television recently that had to do with getting them out. A fourteen-year-old girl called Dorothea came to us. Her mother died in Auschwitz and she never knew what happened to her father. 'Dorry' we called her and she really became part of the family . . . like a young sister to us. She's still in Scotland and we keep in touch.

That was one life-changing commitment. Others took on jobs they would never have dreamed of doing in the ordinary plod of their lives. In the Kyles' case it was that kind of upturn for both husband and wife, and the wider family slotted in to make it possible.

My husband had gone into the Police Reserve . . .

(. . . which considering a youthful contretemps over a game of football in the street was all the more praiseworthy . . .)

So he was called up to the Police and had to leave his work. I took it over and went round all the wee Glasgow shops, the way he'd done, selling Carter's Medical Supplies, castor oil and cough mixture and aspirins, that sort of thing y'know. That was my war work.

Their daughter was sent to school in town and her two grand-fathers collected her day about.

So that was their war work.

Another who served in the police force was Miss Isobel Horn.

I had to be in something, but my father had just died and I thought it would be best if I could volunteer for something that would keep me at home, so I went full-time into the police as a driver . . .

There was Red Cross and W.V.R., pig-food collecting and firewatching. And there was make-do-and-mending: Bunty Angles' aunt turned her own profession to the war effort and made good use of whatever was to hand.

My dressmaker aunt taught make-do-and-mend classes all through the war. Showed folk how to make skirts out of trousers or coats, and children's clothes from adults'.

The weirder the transformation the prouder the transformer.

My dad's plus-fours made matching skirts for me and my twin sister, one from each leg. They were thon scratchy stuff and we hated them, but Mother thought hersel' a rare wee genius and showed them to everybody.

Another whose peacetime skills led naturally to his war work and maybe gave him, quite literally, a step-up in the doing, was Robert Ford.

I had been making wooden barrows for an ironmonger and when the war was coming I got an order from him for twelve thousand wee ladders. Quite rough work. One of these went into every tenement in

Glasgow so people could get up on to roofs through ceiling hatches in case of fire-bombs. I just made them of small trees, eleven or twelve foot long. Cut up the centre, half on each side, and spars between.

All those war efforts were made against a background of increasing complications in just living. Helen Smith had young children to cope with.

Th'was your gas masks of course. You'd aye to have them wi' you at the beginning of the war. You'd Mickey Mouse yins for weans and a big bag-thing you'd to put your baby right inside. We didnae need any of them in the end though, thank goodness. And everb'dy minds of ration books, but d'you mind B.U.s and Points? B.U.s was Bread Units for yon grey kinda bread, and Points was for things that wasnae actu'lly rationed but just short. And mind the queues?

And her neighbour in the lounge minds fine.

Aye, for fish or oranges, and maybe cake from under the counter. But what I was mindin' while you was speakin', Nellie, was yon sticky net you pasted over your windows for 'blast' and the strips of black paper down the sides so's there wasnae chinks in the black-out. Havin' chinks was near as bad as bein' a burglar up our street. And mind how you always took a coupla eggs or a wee bit butter or that, when you went visiting.

There was another tiresome irritation in the black-out. Signposts and station names had been removed and only known landmarks guided travellers.

There were no lights at all when you were going home and you'd to count your stops on the train or the tram or that. That was all to bamboozle enemy parachutists startin' an invasion.

In the event the Glasgow area had just the one deliberate parachutist. Mrs. Jean Walker speaks of him.

My father was an officer in the army but working with the Home Guard. When Hess landed on the farm at Eaglesham they 'phoned my father to ask what to do with him. Then later when Hess was taken to Buchanan Castle my father went out with another officer to interview him before he was taken south. So he'd that conversation with Hess that he always remembered.

If there was only one parachutist there were other less welcome droppings. The blitz came late to Glasgow and for a brief spell. But it was a reign of terror while it lasted. Of course there had been extensive precautions since Day One.

In our church th'was stretchers and Red Cross people at each door, every service, and the stained glass windows was a' boarded up. The closes were made safer wi' props and big sand-baggy walls at the close-mouth. Made them into kinda shelters.

Ann Hutchison's family used their close when the sirens went.

I remember running to the shelter in air raids and jumpin' up and down waitin' for my Daddy. He always seemed to be in the bathroom. The close was all propped up with iron railing kinda things to be stronger. And you'd take your wee bag of money or valuables with you. That wouldnae be much mind.

Most households if they hadn't closes or Anderson shelters had 'safe' places earmarked in their houses and stocked for emergency.

I was a young mother in the Second War and we had a mattress under the stairs. I put my baby in his Moses' basket there and sat beside him all night through the blitz of 1941. Those were bad nights, my husband was in the yard at Fairfield's, then one night a landmine came down by parachute and was tangled on the big crane so that it just dangled there. An incendiary bomb hit the Old South Church in Bearsden too, and it was burned down.

I was lying under our big heavy dining-room table when the bombs fell beside us. What a dunt when one landed at our back, then about five more fell one after the other.

Hamish Thomson was a prisoner-of-war by that time but his home took the second of those dunts.

I heard snatches about the bombing in our area from other prisoners coming in, but didn't really know about it till I came home. What a mess of destruction, with the house wall all propped up waiting for repairs.

All bad enough. But it was Greenock and Clydebank and Govan that took the real devastation, almost obliteration, of those nights. Miss Janet Kay's father worked at Singer's.

> My father walked into Clydebank after the first morning of the blitz there. He met women coming out of Clydebank in their nightdresses, some pushing prams with children and a few belongings. And one of their own men had gone home to find his house and his wife and his children gone. Clydebank was just rubble. But mind you, Singer's had trestle tables out and every employee got his wages that Friday.

Miss Isobel Horn was a canteen van driver at that time.

> I used to drive down to what was left of Clydebank to the docks, taking huge containers of soup and sandwiches to set up a stall.

Mrs. Mary Brisbane lived near the Govan docks.

> One night of the bombing I had my wee son of five wrapped in a blanket in the close. There was a three-storey block of tenement houses across the road from us. There was a direct hit on it and people got thrown down into the dunnies below . . . a lot killed. What a noise there was with the bombs and the rat-tat-tat of ack-ack guns. All our own windows were out and th'was soot and plaster everywhere.

While the armies fought and the air force flew; while grey ships ploughed grey seas and people huddled in shelters, there was a great body of men on both sides . . . prisoners-of-war who spent much of the war champing at the bit, frustrated at being on the sidelines and watching the years of their youth slip past. Let's pick up Hamish Thomson again trundling off on a German motorbike to his monastic sentence. So many things happened that the first few days after that were hazy and confused. Apprehension there must have been, of what was to come, and concern at what the word 'missing' would mean to the family at home. But on that matter there was a providential encounter.

> We were taken somewhere near Paris and we met this girl Bessie Myers who was an ambulance driver and had strayed behind enemy lines. She took our names and addresses in a notebook in case she got back home, and a few weeks later she did go back to Britain and contacted our parents.

If that first stage was hazy, the next one was brutally clear, when the captives were taken on a long week's forced trek to Belgium with other prisoners.

> We'd no rations at all, no food, no water. But as we passed through places, villagers came alongside and gave us bread. Some of us were nearly collapsing from de-hydration.

From Belgium they were transported in railway cattle-trucks to Poland.

> On that train we'd no rations either, but one fellow had got hold . . . somehow or other . . . of a bucket of raw potatoes in water and we survived on that. We were crammed together in that truck, standing . . . couldn't move.

In Poland they registered officially as prisoners-of-war.

> I suppose I must have been about the first R.A.F.V.R. to be captured. Wasn't a great honour that was it? First to be caught! For our rations in Poland we'd roasted acorn coffee for breakfast, watery soup, maybe sauerkraut or potato for lunch, and at night a small loaf among five of us.

After Poland there was Lubeck in Germany, a more comfortable camp with stoves and wooden huts.

> I was one of a group that was caught pinching a better stove from an empty hut . . . got three days' bread and water for that . . . literally bread and water.

Those dreams of commuting home to Britain between sorties, must have seemed very far away, as 1941 slipped into 1942 and 1943. There was Czechoslovakia and the famous Stalagluft 3.

> That's where the big Wooden Horse escape was from, out of the officers section. We used to see them doing their jumping, but we didn't know what it was all about. They got out through the tunnel they'd opened under the vaultinghorse. There was a book about it by one of the ones that got away . . . and then a film.

Lithuania came next . . . and then it was 1945.

The war was nearly over and there was pretty well chaos. We were sent
off roaming around in cattle trucks. Nobody knew where to go. Then
after a week in a big barn somewhere a guard told us just to go, because
the S.S. was coming. So we wandered off . . . just like that! There was
no great dramatic liberation. We met Germans in one village and an
officer wished us luck! We met Americans newly into Europe who'd
never seen uniforms like ours . . . nearly shot us as Germans. From
there we reached Salzburg, Brussels and home. One thing I always
remember. When we got back I could have listened to girls' voices
for ever. That was my war.

He makes light of hard times and talks of another local man with
more startling memories of being a prisoner in Japanese hands and
working in a mine at Hiroshima when the atomic bomb hit the
city.

He was put to clearing up there after the bomb. That must have been
a terrible thing to survive and remember.

Sitting like a bright-eyed sparrow in her suburban nest there's
a dainty little lady touching ninety (and preferring to remain
anonymous) whom it's hard to see as a detainee of war. It wasn't
quite like that but, trapped in Persia with her engineer husband
when 1939 came, she spent the years of the Second War there
'doing her bit' as energetically as she had sold flags for 'gallant
little Montenegro' in the First.

I had been in a dramatic society in Abadan, putting on plays or
pantomimes in peacetime. Well, when the British occupied Abadan
the General asked us to entertain the troops. I sang things from musical
comedies and songs with my banjo and then I did my whistling solos
to my own piano arrangements. I was what they called a 'siffleuse'.
We went on tour . . . oh but it was rough tough travelling . . . to
Basra, Kirkuk, Mosul and Baghdad and into Syria. The young King
of Iraq was there one time when I was singing. It was all hard work.
I once played till my fingers were raw. It was very professional really
. . . great memories.

It's difficult to imagine a less likely siffleuse-banjo player, but
these's a twinkle in the eyes that says it was all a bit of a lark,
that it entertained lonely soldiers, and that if you had to be exiled
anyway, it was best to accept it with devil-may-care gusto.

Back at their ex-patriate homes between theatrical tours, company wives were asked to do another little service for the army authorities, a service that came to nothing . . . absolutely nothing.

There was a general shortage of meat, and trial packs of dried mince (a bit like grapenuts) were sent to the wives to experiment with.

Ali, the cook, had never heard of grapenuts . . .

Food de-hydrated like that mince, if it was good y'see, could be very useful to help move army food supplies easily. Anyway, I was up early and left my package in the pantry. When I came in later I didn't see it so I asked Ali, four foot-nothing and temperamental, where he'd put it.

'Memsahib, I plant it . . . plenty flowers . . . plenty 'sturtium. Come.'

And he took me to the garden and sure enough there were drills and drills planted out neatly with mince.

'That's meat you've planted, Ali.'

He looked pityingly for what the sun had done to me.

'Oh, Memsahib, too many hot season.' He shook his head.

'These *seeds* for the garden.'

But when Memsahib and her husband finally came home it was neither nasturtium or sprouting mince that the homesick couple gloried in.

It was the Scottish gardens along the shore with wee rows of green cabbages that we saw through our binoculars as we came up the Clyde . . . then we knew we were home.

Mr. Angelo Lamarra had a strange war for a Stenh'smuir supporter, born here and on sunny terms with all his Glasgow café customers.

The very day the Italians came into the war in 1940 we'd a brick through the café window. It was shattering in more ways than one. We'd been brought up friends with everyone, and-here all of a sudden we were enemies. I was alone in the café when that brick came through the window and I was trembling. Two men came in and looked at me. I was quite fair, so one of them says, he says, 'He's no' a Tally.' And they went away. The police came and just stood around watching for any more trouble. Gangs of lads were just roaming around looking for Italian cafés. Anyway, that very night my brother and I were arrested. They had our names from the 'Casa', the Italian club. It was s'posed to be

Fascist, but it wasnae Fascist at all. We were all Scottish really, just getting together with each other. Italians are like that. Besides we'd registered for the British army ten days before. Och, it was all a right mix-up. One of the friends I've played golf with for years was in the Italian army.

They were sorted out in Edinburgh. 'Just moved about like chessmen y'know' then taken south to the docks for shipping out to Canada as internees.

We saw two ships at the dock. They filled up the *Arandora Star* first. (It was torpedoed and went down with all of them.) Then we were put on the *Ettrick Star* and zig-zagged across the Atlantic to the St. Lawrence. We were put on an island near Montreal. Didn't see a woman all the time we were there, except someone had binoculars and you could see girls walking across the bridge that way. We wore sort of blue uniforms with red stripes up the trousers and a red circle on your back.

But it's a small world even in war.

The Canadian guards pushed us around a bit . . . thought we were Germans. Then one of them shouted,
  'Anyone here speak English?'
  'Aye of course we do, half of us are from Glasgow.'
  'You're kidding' says this big Canadian. 'I was born at Parkhead!'
After that we were well-treated all the years we were there. We came back to the Isle of Man before the end of the war, then did a bit of what they called 'work of national importance'. Then it was home and back to the café again. Wasn't bad my internment, just kind of silly and sad. But that's war!

Jimmy Dewar shared the deck of his rescue ship with German prisoners and Greek survivors from another ship.

The Greeks were always at daggers drawn with the Germans, but we found the Jerries O.K. We played cards with them and they talked about how sure they were to win the war . . . sink everything and have their armies all over. We listened, but just went on dealing the cards.

He doesn't mention though, whether the Germans were as 'model' at sea as Helen Thomson saw them with the female eye on land.

I was in a camp for a while alongside a German P.O.W. compound. Never saw anything so neat and tidy and well-looked after . . . everything ticketty-boo y'know. Quite outshone the British section or any other camp I ever saw.

But in the end maybe the slappier-happier allied ways fired their energies better for the final outcome. And while no victory ever prevents people being displaced, lost, or even massacred to tidy them out of the way, the Glasgow war wanderers who remembered for these pages, finally took up their blessedly humdrum lives again. They melted back into grey suits and family life so that younger generations can scarcely imagine them as quarter-mistresses, fighter-pilots or grim-faced men with bayonets and machine-guns, or see genial Stop-Me-and-Buy-One ice-cream men as dangerous enemy aliens.

16

There was None of this Sex or that in Those Days

The years when little boys pull their jerseys over their hands to avoid the contamination of actually taking little girls' hands in school circle games, are soon over. They pass quickly into the 'looking over' stage . . . days when egos are easily bruised and hearts broken. Norma Morton remembers their bitter sweetness . . . with a twinkle in her eye.

> I thought I was lovely when I was at school. Here's me wi' my forty-two inch bust and my long hair that I used to throw over my shoulder all the time and toss my head . . . kind of flirty . . . y'know the way. But here I knew that I wasnae really lovely . . . just fat . . . fat! I used to think I'd be thin when I grew up right, because grown-ups didn't eat sweets.

With families of nine and ten you might think there was little need for sex education, that regular arrivals of midwives and clash in the close would have told them all they needed to know. But it wasn't invariably so. Mrs. Chrissie Ronnie remembers.

> My mother was too busy with the farm and shop, and the family of course, to tell me anything about life. But I always remember just before she died, when I was thirteen coming up fourteen, she told me I shouldn't play so much with the boys. Then she lifted my arm and stretched it out.
>
> 'Chrissie, see how long your arm is there? Well, never let the boys past your finger tips!'
>
> They wouldnae like that nowadays, would they?

And her sister too, one of the twelve Rodgers, looks back on primmer days.

Some say 'good old days', some say 'bad old days', I don' know. There was none of this sex or that, and if you were seen going in or out a pub in those days with a man . . . well! Nowadays they're *floating* in and out.

There's ample evidence that it *was* a more innocent day . . . polite too. One rememberer recalls hearing of a girl having a young woman pointed out to her in company as being lesbian, and then in later conversation with the young lady in question . . .

. . . asking, friendly-like, 'And whit-part of Lesbia d'you come fae?'

Alas for such naiveté.

There were mating rites of course, the stalking and the chase. One gentleman was not prepared to kiss and tell.

We went to the pictures right-enough when we were coortin' (winchin' we called it, no'coortin'). Forbye that it's a secret.

But Mrs. Agnes Grove was more forthcoming, and looks back nearly eighty years to how it was in her day.

Th'were places you walked on Saturday and Sunday looking for a chap. We walked up and down at the canal where the locks were . . . some girls did it at Alexandra Parade. Boys did the same . . . 'looking for a lumber' they called it. And they used to sit on the canal wall too, the boys and girls.

Jack Roche and his peers had another beat.

You could meet wi' clicks at the Park bandstand. You kinda walked about outside the railing lookin' each other up and down. When you were serious wi' one you took her inside . . . *and paid*. That was dead serious.

In Italian circles Mario Servadei recalls, there was a touch more formality.

Y'know folk talk about arranged marriages? Italians didn't exactly arrange them, when I was young, but when you visited other families on Sundays they maybe put you in the way of each other if they thought it was suitable. Maybe left the young folks in a room with a gramophone or that. . . and waited to see if a date came out of that. And of course there was always the dancing on a Thursday night at

Green's Ballroom. That was the night all the Italians went . . . just a thing that happened. About the actual weddings . . . well, in Italy there'd have been dowries . . . specially southern Italy, but that didn't last beyond the first generation here.

In Jewish circles between the wars it wasn't pounding the clicking beat, or Green's dancing that brought the young together; it was the Jewish Institute in South Portland Street, a social rendez-vous for the immigrant community.

My husband Solly was a staunch member of the Institute and I met him there. When we were getting married he was offered the use of a room. So the canopy (you know how we're married under a canopy with flowers up the corner poles) well, it was brought from the synagogue, and we'd the breaking of the glass and all the symbols for long and happy married life. After the wedding Mrs. Geneen, who was a great caterer, did the purvey. She was a real benefactor to couples who hadn't a lot of money . . . didn't take much at all. It's all big presents now y'know, videos and dishwashers . . . but not then. Somebody would play an instrument or sing and entertain at these old traditional weddings.

Sometimes it was at work that people took a fancy to each other. Mrs. Grove found her partner that way.

I met my husband at the Templeton's factory. He was a tenter. Tenters kept an eye on the looms, hooked up your pieces and watched in case things went wrong. He came into the factory to help get the looms back to doing the chenille, after they'd been put to making the army blankets in the First War.

And another claimed that her work romance had a touch of *The People's Friend* about it.

I worked in a big store when I was young, right after the First War, about 1919. I thought I was a bit of a catch wi' my hair up an' my nice blouses. And so must've Alec in Gents' Suits. He kep' asking me out. He was quite pan-loaf spoken, y'know . . . dark wavy hair and a wee moustache (wee moustaches was just comin' in). Anyway when Bert the doorman seen him chattin' me up, he says, 'You mind what you're doin' wi' that Alec. He's maybe a heid-bummer in Gents, but I wouldnae trust him wi' a window dummy.' Bert was just a wee nyaff and I didnae pay any heed. But I didnae marry Alec. It was him really was the wee nyaff. I got wed in the end to Bert. It was just a poke of sweeties and the pictures when we went out. Bert did me fine though, for forty-two year.

She could count her honest-woman anniversaries, but another rememberer wasn't so sure . . .

. . . married eleven years. Or d'you count the common-law years afore we got wed?

So for some those days were maybe not so innocent, but Peggy Carson recalls one relationship that clearly was.

I went to see a weddin' once at a chapel in the east end and th'was some women standin' watchin' the bride go in.
'She's no' expectin' y'ken.'
'No' expectin'. That's posh for you, sure it is.'

A virtuous ceremony like that must surely have been preceded by a douce courtship, like the wooing and winning of Mary Rodger.

There was no what you'd call 'courting' done with Mr. Brisbane. He lived just over the road from us. It was just 'hello' and that. And then he began to come about the house and do this and that to help us. It was just every second Sunday or Monday after seven o'clock we went for walk, and maybe very occasionally the pictures. I was in service for a wee while and he came to see me there. We were married in the wee church up in Scotland Street. I was in a blue dress with a blue hat and my going-away coat was blue with braid round it and a very pale blue cloche hat. We just had our tea at home and then our honeymoon in Ireland. I was married fifty-seven years.

Mrs. Mysie Kyle also favoured blue for her wedding outfit, perhaps surprisingly not *navy* blue with a white trimmed pill-box.

My brother was a great one for the football and I met my husband when he came up with his Boys' Brigade footballers to Blochairn Church. They trained in our cellar. It was a big cellar. Anyway when the teams were playing near-at-hand I took out the oranges at half-time and met him like that. He used to come to the Bible Class too. We'd a quiet wedding at the manse and I wore a blue frock with a bolero, and a hat I made myself that had roses on it the same as my bouquet.

They went to Girvan for the week-end, but Mr. Kyle was too far-ben with the B.B. to make it more.

> We came home and took the B.B. to camp at Tighnabruaich. Yes, the honeymoon was the B.B. camp, but we enjoyed it fine. We'd our holidays for years at the camp after that.

Ann Hutchison viewed her sister's Pollokshaws courtship with interest.

> When Jeanie had her boyfriend they used to sit in the hut where my Daddy kept the wood for his cart. Jeannie always sawed up that wood and chopped the sticks. No pictures for them. They just lit the lamp in that hut and sat splitting the wood . . . done their courting over them sticks. She worked hard, Jeanie. And then there was the bobby going round on his beat. When he seen the lamp lit he would come in the hut for his cup of tea from the wee stove.

Like those others, Mrs. Bunty Angles' wedding to her baker-suitor, John, was an all-Glasgow affair. He was a City Bakeries man, and there was a new C.B. restaurant in Partick.

> It was in Byres Road . . . Peel House it was, and big Willie Urie says to John, 'How about getting married in our new hall. Give it a nice opening.' So we did. It was lovely. I wore a white lace dress gored with georgette, 'bought'. And I'd a wee cap and veil with a cluster of bride's blossom at my ears.

She wasn't so pleased though, with her going-away hat.

> It was to go with my outfit and it was orange and brown pan velvet . . . My, it was big! Great big brim. If ever you saw anything ridiculous it was that hat. A daft thing to go in the train to Stonehaven with.

Not all courtships were boy-and-girl next-street or neighbourhood affairs. Robert Ford went a-wooing in Kilmarnock where a chance introduction had brought him an embarrassment of riches in the bevy of seven bonnie sisters from among whom he found his wife. 'Spoilt for choice he was,' she claims. There was maybe a near miss though.

> He'd an old highland girl friend, Flora, who was a very good dancer and very keen on it, and I've said to him many a time, 'You know if you could've danced as well as that Angus that did get her, he wouldn't have had a look-in with Flora.'

So maybe young Mr. Ford did better to occupy himself making his hods and bakers' trays than pay for ten lessons at McEwans' Dancing and end up with the wrong wife . . .

Kilmarnock in earlier days was a fair stretch to go a-wooing, but some relationships were conducted at even greater distances. This one began quite conventionally in Glasgow.

> I met my husband at The Plaza in 1926. I was at a friend's twenty-first birthday party. John was home on leave from British petroleum in Persia and he'd been persuaded to come to this party. That's how we met and all his leave we were very chummy.

There was no rush though.

> I was courted from Persia really. I met him in 1926 and he was home again to get married in 1935. Nine years . . . no hurry. I was very busy with other interesting things to do. We went to Persia after the wedding.

Angelo Lamarra's romance looked like following good Italian-Glasgow traditions, but the war and separation tested it.

> My wife had come over from Italy when she was twelve to help in the family shop when her older brothers were away at the First War. She still speaks with an accent. It's nice that. I admired her for a long time at the Italian Club, but then we met properly. We played tennis and went to films, and we danced at the Locarno and the Albert. 1/6 at the Plaza too, in an afternoon. Louis Freeman's band. For the pictures we went to the La Scala . . . wee cups of tea in the side seats, y'know.

(A well integrated Italian-Scot, Angelo Lamarra, to refer to *the* La Scala!)

> But then I was interned in Canada for the war. Interrupted everything. But she worked hard at home and had a wee business ready for us. We kept writing and I came out the camp in April and we got married in the July. Didn't waste any more time. She and I get on great. We've one wee argument every day . . . over nothing. If we don't have that I start worrying.

Perhaps, although it's related at second-hand, we should end the chapter with the most exotic, and eventually doomed, romance, that of the wooing and marriage of Mr. Alan Dale's father.

Short-lived it may have been, but there is no doubt that he was head-over-heels in love.

My father was born in 1873. He ran away to sea at twelve on a ship called *Gipsy Maid*. He worked in America for a year or two and then he was back to sea. On one voyage he met a girl from a circus and the only way he could stay with her was to join the circus. She was with a trapeze family so he learned to be a trapeze artist too. He was very young and off they went round the world with Talbot-Cook's circus. They'd a daughter, a trapeze artist too . . . my half-sister. That first wife died of blackwater fever in Sumatra.

Wooings, weddings and honeymoons, romance. And reality. For it wasn't every woman who found her honeymoon on the highlight of her life and Mrs. Norma Morton remembers a fellow-patient in hospital, disgruntled at the prospect of going home.

'I don't want to go home. I want to stay here,' she says. 'The food's good and it's clean. It's been better'n my honeymoon I tell you that.'

17
D'you Mind the Penny Geggie?

Whatever their deprivations Glasgow people have always had a reputation for enjoying themselves. And never more than in the Edwardian and later days covered by this book, coming as they did close on the heels of Victorian Presbyterian times when public entertainment was a decidedly suspect frivolity. Of course there was great theatre and music-hall last century, but it was not wholly approved by Kirk and Session who witheringly minuted such ongoings as 'theatricals'.

But the hoi-poloi liked its theatricals, as it later loved its 'pictures' in the days when Glasgow became Cinema City with over a hundred picture-houses. The taste for performance showed itself early in life and even organisations dedicated to moral uplift had begun to grasp the revolutionary notion that fun and games could go quite sinlessly with precept.

> I used to be in the church kinderspiel. That would be before the First War. Kinderspiels were wee kind of children's musicals.
>
> We used to go to the Rechabite kinderspiels in Dennistoun. I loved that but I was too shy to actually be in one.

Not so other stage-struck tots.

> I was an angel in the kinderspiel and I mind Miss Duckett at the piano with her long-long earrings that used to jingle when she plonked out the tunes. She'd a long neck and a red nose, but she could fairly bash out the songs.

Mrs. Lily Balarsky was fascinated by theatre long before she was old enough to have a ticket and sit on a plush seat. It was her *elbows* that sat on the velvet.

You know about 'hings'? Well, when we were young and living in Stockwell Street people had wee cushions at their windows to lean on when they hung out to have a chat or just watch the passing show. We'd an orange-box to stand on and look across into the dressing-rooms of the old Metropole Theatre. It was great . . . very glamorous to see the show-biz folk getting changed and the girls sharing a wee puff. That shocked me, it was so wicked. We saw them pulling up their tights too. That was good for a giggle.

Sometimes the thrill of living so close to the Metropole was almost heart-stopping.

We used to stand in the lane at the stage-door and see them *in the flesh* coming in. There was a Jewish performer . . . what was his name? Yes, Ike Freeman, he was good, and there was G.H. Elliot, the Chocolate-Coloured Coon. He was lovely at the stage-door. We just stood there and got a wee pat on the head.

The day did come when Lily was actually *inside*.

My older brother got a wee job with the ice-cream and sweetie tray. We thought we were practically *in* the profession. I remember getting in at the back to watch Gertie Gitana shimmying around the stage and singing . . .
　　'How do you feel when you marry your ideal?
　　Ever so goosey, goosey, goosey . . . gooo-sey.'
And the audience all joined in.

Many a later theatre or cinema-goer served an apprenticeship at what they called the Penny Geggie.

D'you mind of Penny Geggies? Och, I fair loved the Penny Geggie. It was a wee kinda portable magic-lantern that came round the schools or the street, and you got in for a ha'penny.

If the likes of the Geggie was no longer a Victorian sin, Isobel Horn made a moral lapse out of its arrival at her local school.

I wasn't at school yet, but this man they called 'French Geggie' was coming with his show to the playground. I wanted to go and it was arranged that the maid at my friend Jean's house would take us. So I got my penny. But-here Lizzie couldn't take us and we just went ourselves. I knew I shouldn't but I did. Well, when we got to the playground it was all over and the Geggie barrow covered up. So the bold Jean led me astray a bit more and we went to Clements' shop on the main road and *spent* the penny. Mrs. Clement was a wee fat lady in a black dress. Anyway, did I not get lalldie when they found out at home?

Another glimpse of the show and its admission charge . . .

. . . A Geggie-man hurled his cart, and a monkey with it, round near us, and you paid a bottle to see his moving-picture show . . . great!

The Penny Geggie stuck to streets and playgrounds, but buskers penetrated the closes into back courts and were a source, not only of entertainment, but also of inspiration to imitate.

We'd great people coming round. There was a hurdy-gurdy man and there was one lot always started off with 'I'll sing a hymn to Mary'. Then if it wasn't a very Catholic tenement they went on to 'The Old Rugged Cross'. There was a coloured man too, came to Parson Street (there weren't many coloured folk around at that time so he was quite exotic) he used to come with a horn gramophone on a pram, and you threw your pennies out the window. He looked quite poor but they said he left a lot of money.

Alex Donnelly was on the receiving end of the pennies for a time.

Things were bad in the slump. We'd no work. Even my fiddle was in the pawn. I got together with a friend that was a good singer and got the lend of wee Willie Spraggan's fiddle and went busking. We went to Paisley first where nob'dy knew us. We didn't make much, but enough to get my fiddle out the pawn. I went on my own after that and did better. Eventually I went all over Ireland . . . knew the purser on the Irish boat and got over for five shillings. Played for the passengers on the way over. When I got a job back in Glasgow again I chummed up wi' an accordionist and we went out on Saturday afternoons to make a bit extra.

There's scarcely a rememberer of tenement days who didn't emulate the buskers and hold their own back-green concerts. Eileen Reilly was prominent (in a refined way) in their troupe.

Great these concerts were. I couldn't sing so I used to say poetry. Mind you, my father had taught me how to whistle. But my mother was indignant. It was not ladylike to whistle and the idea of me doing it in public had her speechless. There's a saying 'The two things God hates most are a crowing cock and a whistling hen.' So God and my mother had the same idea. Anyway, the kids from the other closes would come to your concert and pay a penny. There'd be your singers and reciters and some that did their dancing-class dances.

Such concerts were often charitable efforts . . .

. . . maybe for a book or a game for someone in hospital. That was very unselfish because it was usually the fever, and everything got burned so you couldn't get a shot of it after.

At our concerts they paid at the close-mooth, then came through and sat on the ground. I always mind one hefty wench Bridie Cooney, covered and jinglin' wi' medals doin' Irish dancin'. Light as a feather too, she was.

Down on the back-greens after dark, other unwitting, in-house entertainment was provided by the midgey-men on their rounds.

I used to watch them from the window if I couldnae sleep. They came round with lamps on their heids for the dark and made a right racket clattering the bins. And woe betid you if it had of been your job to bring in the clo'es line that day, for the midgeys wi' baskets on their back, would just take their knife and slash the rope to get by . . . they'd of got their throat strangled if they'd walked into it. We'd midgey-rakers too, lookin' for treasures.

Not a fat living in days when every ha'penny was looked at twice and every article used till it was worthless, then fliped and used again.

Then it was on to the Big-Time . . . real, paying shows, although some future stars had got their start right there in the back-courts.

Some of your back-green singers went on to be proper music-hall turns (maybe no' always that proper), and some got started in wee local shows. Will Fyffe, Harry Lauder and Harry Gordon did their early stand-up comic turns in these wee Glasgow halls.

And then there were the 'filums'. Nothing about those very early shows, the bioscope and the quick 'shorts' suggested the popular rage that cinemas would shortly become.

Film came in as a novelty with a hand-cranked projector. Sometimes it was just a wee extra at the circus.

Alan Dale (later Glasgow cinema manager) had that straight from
the clown's mouth, so to speak.

> I know that because my father was in the circus then, at the turn of the
> century. After the trapeze thing he clowned with his saxophone. He
> was the one who told me that they used to put up a screen for a short
> film as one of the items on the programme.

From being a 'flash-in-the-pan' novelty 'the pictures' soon became
a part of everyday life and certain names and cinemas began to be
household words, certainly in the Roche home.

> When I was very wee th'was the Electric Theatre in Argyle Street (no'
> the Eglinton Electreum. That was Eglinton Street) and th'were the
> Panopticon in the Trongate . . . used to be the Britannia Music Hall.
> I always remember seein' Stan Laurel in his first film there.

Some recall those two halls with affection, others with shocked
awe.

> I always remember my brother taking me there. My, it was a wild
> place! It was yon German one, Marlene Dietrich. In this film she'd
> gone into the water and all her clothes were sticking to her. I was
> very embarrassed.

But Glasgow flocked to see Marlene and her like, skuddy or not.
And by the 'twenties picture-houses were mushrooming . . .
fancy sophisticated palaces in the city, a plethora of back-street
bug-houses, and small cinemas between the two.

> A lot of early cinemas were just built in back-courts of tenements
> and came through to the front on to the street. They said the City
> Fathers approved of this because the pictures should be where the
> people were. There was an idea that when the cinema came there
> was less drunkenness.

Some of those were the kind that Mr. Bill Bain recalls.

> When I was wee there was a picture house that I thought was called the
> Matinee. It was really the Crownie. It was bench seats and they used
> to grab you under the oxters and shift you along to get more in. You
> tried to spread your bottom out to get more space. There was another
> place called the B. B. Wellington Palace and you got in for a penny on

Saturday afternoons. The manager there was a big-big giant and he'd a long pole he poked you with to close up in the queue.

In the cinema's heydey there were eleven big cinemas in the city centre square mile, with outwardly radiating circles to the furthest suburbs. In Shawlands three miles out, an inner suburb no more than a mile long and a furlong wide, there were seven. Ann Hutchison remembers them all.

Sometimes I went to the Wee Pollok beside the river. Then Mr. Noble had his place that was a mixture of music-hall turns and wee films. Wasn't really his. He just looked after it. There was a wee toty hall between Shawlands Cross and Minard Road. No' many people mind of it. And th'was the Camphill behind the Marlborough. The big ones was the Waverley, the Embassy (it was newer) and the Elephant. D'you mind the wee lit-up elephant outside that used to toss up his trunk wi' the wee umbrella on the top:

I used to go a lot to the pictures in Shawlands . . . Jeanette MacDonald in her crinolines and Nelson Eddy and Rudolph Valentino. It was historical films in old-fashioned clo'es that I liked the best.

But they weren't everyone's favourite. Some who had a surfeit of those costume dramas moaned at the prospect of more.

Och, no' another of them filums where the guy writes wi' a feather! I like Westerns.

That cinema heydey is long gone now, but memories of it linger with the likes of Lily Joseph.

I liked the pictures in the days of Douglas Fairbanks and Mary Pickford, Gloria Swanson . . . good clean pictures. I went regular. But it must be ten years now since I saw a film, except on the television and they're not always very nice.

Some, like Janet Kay, thought they were a cut above the cinema and preferred the genteel ambience of the theatre, though they defected occasionally.

Oh yes, for Spencer Tracy. *Anything* with Spencer Tracy. But mostly it was theatre. My friend and I thought we were a bit superior going to the Brandon Thomas rep. and the opera. Mind you it was just the gods. We would be earning about eighteen shillings a week at the time. You knew everybody in the gods . . . not their names right-enough, but you spoke to them week by week.

There were audience skills and techniques early learned by theatre-goers. You didn't just shuffle in, show your ticket and sit quietly down. Oh dear no!

> When it was the opera you'd been standing in the queue eating your sandwich. Then the doors opened and you went belting up the stair, because it was 1/6d 'early doors' and 2/3d 'ordinary doors'. 'Early doors' you got your choice of seats. When they played the National Anthem at the beginning you could always tell the regulars because they sat down at the beginning of the last line to get their bottoms on the bench first . . . the rest had to wiggle theirs in between as best they could. It was hot too. You sat fair steamin' up there in the gods.

When the Brandon Thomas Players folded, the two drama addicts graduated to permanent weekly seats for his successor, Wilson Barratt . . .

> . . . and you went dressed with your best coat and hat, and your handbag under your arm. You wouldn't have *insulted* Wilson Barrett or Richard Matthews by going casual. You'd your tea at the interval too. Oh, we werenae-half ladies by then! The company had Kitty de Legh and Phyllis Barker, George Larchet and Simon Lack (when he was still just Alex McAlpine from Tollcross). I had a real crush on Wilson Barrett. Oh my, they were terr-ific, wonderful!

Lily Balarsky had graduated from her 'peeping teenie' days across to the Metropole, and become an enthusiast for the drama too.

> Early in the century there was a group of Yiddish players used to go round . . . travelling players performing Jewish plays, mostly Yiddish. They came to the Princess's Theatre and the immigrants flocked to see them. They didn't get paid much and they'd to rely on Jewish families to give them hospitality. Dalnikoffs, the leather merchants, were one family that was specially good at giving them lodgings. Later there were the Avrom Greenbaum Players. They didn't just stick to Jewish plays, but a lot of them were.

Not everyone had the money to be regulars at theatre or cinema and when hard times came even those who had managed an occasional night out had empty pockets. But sometimes help was at hand.

> During the General Strike in 1926 there were special free concerts for the workers. My father was a railwayman on strike and I went with him to one of these in a hall somewhere. I always remember a man singing 'Rocked in the Cradle of the Deep'.

Cheek by jowl with the eleven big cinemas and nine theatres in that central Glasgow mile, there were ten dance halls, for Glasgow was one of the hoppingest, skippingest, Palais Gliding cities in Europe between the wars. Indeed it claims that, for its dance-halls and other entertainments 95% of all Americans on leave in Britain in the Second War came at some time to Glasgow. Young Glasgow was serious about its dancing.

> When I was young, coming up a bit, we used to go to McEwan's Dancing Class in Pollokshields Burgh Hall, so when you went to the Plaza, you could do it.

Bunty Angles studied the steps and picked them up as she went along. She too favoured the Plaza, though not always.

> On Saturday nights I went to the dancing. You were working late in the shop so you went straight there . . . had your dancing shoes at work with you, and something for your tea. Or maybe John, my young man, would bring them when he came to meet me. There was the Plaza for big nights out and tea-dances in the afternoon, if John's shifts fitted in.

Tuesday afternoon being what they called in Glasgow 'the half-shut-day' for big stores, shop workers trooped to the afternoon Plaza.

> An' if your fella wasnae off-shift you just danced wi' your China.

That wasn't for Bunty Angles though.

> The Plaza was nice with the coloured fountains and wee tables. John and I liked it there. But we went to the F. and F. Palais in Partick too, and Green's Playhouse, the Locarno, and the Albert in thingummy street. It was the Lancers and the Charleston then with your legs all kicking and twisting from the knees. Later it was foxtrots and waltzes. I loved the dancing.

Providing some of the music for the dancing craze was that resilient Victorian, Alan Dale's father. From runaway sailor to trapeze-man to clown, he turned to straight music with his saxophone.

> He got a band together and played for gigs and for the dancing. Must've been quite old then, but the bands began to go out and, in the end, he and my mother just ran a boarding-house for actors and music-hall people.

Alex Donnelly, now ninety, still plays a lively fiddle, saxophone and keyboard, up in his own eyrie in a high-rise flat, but in his day he too played for the 'jigging'.

> Sometimes you got dressed up wi' your bow tie an'that, when it was a late-night dance or a wedding at the Marlborough or the Grosvenor. You just took every job you could get.

There was music in the parks too, at the bandstands where the young hovered looking for their clicks. Struan Yule's local bandstand was in Alexandra Park.

> May to September the bands played there. The notices said *WEDNESDAYS and FRIDAYS, D.V. and W.P.* There were Dixie Minstrels too and a troupe called 'Song Salad'.

The young still dance and listen to their music, watch their drama. To an older generation their pleasures are almost incomprehensible . . . to those reared on neat little shoe-bags, formal steps and small courtesies, their dancing seems wild and disjointed, their music raucous. But it is *theirs*, and half-a-century from now, they will surely look back as we do, with tenderness and laughter at the seriousness with which they took the entertainment of their youth.

18

Tennis Bats and Golf Sticks

We promised young Christina in an earlier chapter that while there would be precious few more tomboy games in the street, there would surely be a diversion or two in and around the house for a thirteen-year-old with a tribe of brothers and sisters to 'mother'. Roaming far from home was over but you could still do your five-stones.

> Aye, I'd run for miles with my gir' in my young days, but then, after, it was things like chuckies. I mind being in Craigton Cemetery one day with Chrissie . . . down to see our mother's grave . . . and-here, we saw the place where they did the grave-stones.
> 'Come on' says I. 'See if he'll make us chuckies'.
> 'I'm no' going to make you chuckies,' says he.
> 'Well that's tellin' me straight,' says I.
> 'If I mak' you chuckies, that wee lass there'll want chuckies, and then you'll go and tell some others and I'll have a queue at my door for chuckies'.
> He didn't know Chrissie was my sister. So we didnae get the nice marble chuckies . . . just had to play with wee stones.

Chuckies were versatile, you could carry them in your pocket, play them indoors or out and there was no particular shape they had to conform to. Everyone had them. But some better than others.

> You could just play wi' wee stones, but I had awful nice chuckies. They were an inch square maybe, and corri-gated. Four of them, a white, a brown, a green and a red, and you'd your jaurie on the floor. You'd to throw them up and before they came down, pick up the jaurie and see how many of your chuckies you could catch.

Children of an earlier age were more familiar with what might lurk in their hair . . . even in heads where the pigtails were

excruciatingly tight, pulled back so hard that the temples rose
in itchy lumps. So the rhyme that went with some games of
five-stones was not the insult it might seem in the 1990s.

> See the wee beasts in your heid
> See the tate in mine
> See the wee beasts in your heid
> See there's nane in mine!

That last line came from Jack Roche with the triumphant shout that
meant carpet or pavement was clear of chuckies. Even at ninety-
odd, Mrs. Agnes Grove can think wistfully of her set of stones.

> I wasn't good at them mind. They used to fall off my hand. But I often
> wish I'd kept my chuckies. They were nice.

Playing shops was another indoor/outdoor pastime and
especially engrossing when like Miss Isobel Horn, you stocked
your own store.

> I used to sit on the back step and champ down wee bits of sandstone
> into smithereens or powder. If the stone was white that would be sugar
> or sugar lumps, or maybe cheese. If it was red, that might be mince. I
> liked 'shops'.

Then there were the collections. You might be in a room-and-
kitchen or a single-end . . .

> . . . but there was aye room for your scraps, losh me, aye! Or maybe
> later your foreign stamps. I kept my scraps in a Coronation tin . . .
> George the Fifth it would be. Was that about 1911? I'd angels and
> fancy ladies, and some big baskets of flowers that you could change
> for a whole-lot of wee scraps from other people . . . enough to cover
> yours to make the bargain fair.

For boys one of the favourite collections was of cigarette cards.

> D'you minda cigarette cards eh? 'Hey Mister, gaunnie gie's your
> cigarette photie?' You used to watch for men takin' out their fags
> . . . workmen an' that. I'd a lot of sets, battles and footballers and
> inventions. And one time th'was wee silk flags and wild flowers . . .
> Kensitas that was. They were nice.

There were young capitalists of course, who collected money, as entrepreneurs with small businesses in lemonade bottles, or as fire-goys to Jewish neighbours. And, like John Adamson, they often banked their takings.

> I loved my Golliwog bank. You're no' allowed to say that now, but if you knew how much I liked that nigger-bank you'd know it was a love-name. He was metal and he'd a red enamel jersey, and he had a bent arm wi' an open hand you put your penny in. Then you pushed down a wee stubby lever behind his shoulder and the hand came up to his big open mouth so's the penny got swallowed. There was a grating on the bottom you unscrewed to get at your money.

But however much the bank, any bank . . . was loved, there was no showing him off.

> You werenae allowed to bring it out in front of your aunts or uncles or visitors for fear they would think you were cadging for money.

Stamps and chess and dominoes were for the patient and painstaking and in the 'teen years of the century and again in the thirties, there was another craze that delighted those who could wait for results.

> I once had a goldfish that died and we'd a lovely funeral and everything for him. But-here I was awful upset and it was my granny said I should make a coalie-plant in the bowl. You put in bits of coal in the bottom and then you sprinkled on the top some wee bits of chemicals that she sent me to Ogg's the chemist for. After a few days it grew lovely fl'rescent mould in all different colours and patterns. I wish't I could get that recipe again. It was beautiful.

So, wet days and winter nights, there was plenty to do indoors. They played houses and hospitals, schools and shops and concerts. They made makeshift cots and prams and chairs for the dolls that were their babies and patients, pupils, customers and audiences. Alison Dow had two particular dolls.

> One was just stuffed and had a cloth face and I played with her all the time. She wasn't bonnie but I loved her. The other was beautiful. She had a china face, nice yellow hair and jointed legs. She'd a green velvet coat with fur trims and a fur hat. I only played with her when we'd visitors or on Sundays . . . or sometimes I got to bring her out when we were playing houses and we needed her to be the minister's wife.

Most dolls had names but Peggy Carson's was a modern mystery-miss from overseas.

> I'd a doll that came from my auntie in America. That would be about 1920. She'd an Eton crop and long-long legs. (No' my auntie . . . the doll!) She'd a blue wardrobe with hangers and a whole-lot of clothes in it. She was different from other dolls. But, funny thing, I never had a name for her.

There were other little mothers who had to do without real dolls and adapt dish-mops, dressing them up with handkerchiefs and copying-ink faces. Some few like the little Rodgers had no dolls.

> Och no! We'd no toys at all. We certainly hadn't a doll in the house. No money for that sort of thing.

They did have hens in the back court that others might have envied. They had a real house too, and a real shop out-front. But there the play was all too earnest.

> You see, at thirteen, I was in the house . . . and my sister, at a wee bit older, ran the shop.

They don't do too much learning by rote nowadays, not even much learning of poetry to recite for a sweetie or a gold star on a Friday afternoon. But maybe it was that old abandoned practice that spawned all the counting-out rhymes we've looked at elsewhere, or that gave birth to singing games, maybe even produced the chants for being as rude as they dared in Edwardian times when they hurled insults at offending peers.

Singing games could be played in street, playground or backyard (or at parties if the family finances ran to 'sangwidges', reading-sweeties, jellies and iced gems). Of some of the games only the jingles are remembered now, What was this for . . . ball . . . skipping?

> Hey, gee-up my cuddy
> My cuddy ower the dyke
> And if you touch my cuddy
> My cuddy'll gie you a bite.

Or this obscure story?

> My mither mendit my auld breeks
> And wow! They were a–diddy-o
> She sent me to get Mally shod
> At Robbie Tamson's smiddy-o
> The smiddy staun's ayont the burn
> That wimples through the clachan
> There's ne'er a time that I pass by
> But whit I fa' to lachin'-o

They may not know what that meant but, to a man or woman, they can tell you how to play Bee-Baw-Babbity, Water Water Wallflower and Queen Mary.

> Water water wallflower, growing up so high
> We are all maidens and we must all die
> Excepting Carrie Grossmith, the youngest of us all
> She can dance, and she can sing, and she can knock us all down.
> Fie, fie, fie-fie shame, turn your face to the wall again.

> Queen, Mary, Queen Mary, my age is sixteen
> My father's a farmer in yonder green
> He's plenty of money to dress me in silk
> But there's nae bonnie laddie will tak' me awa'

More of a street game, since it called for outdoor space, was Eely Ally-o

> There's a big ship sailing through the Eely Ally-o
> The Eely Ally-o, the Eely Ally-o
> There's a big ship sailing through the Eely Ally-o
> On the nine-*teenth*-of-De*cem*-ber.

You played that all joined in a line behind a leader wi' her's arm makin' an arch against the wall. Then the rest went under till you were in a tight curl, then you'd unwind . . . singin' away all the time.

'Singing-games' . . . the very words conjure up a picture of merry innocence . . . a romp of little girls in crisp pinafores, woollen stockings and tammies, or small boys in button-bunnets, playing happily like sanitised children in a pantomime with never a sour note. The truth is, of course, that they rejoiced in rude little rhymes, sang corrupted versions of their 'nice' songs and threw

venomous insults at each other with even more enthusiasm. One
just had to trill two parody-lines of a popular classic to have a sarky
reply from another to match it.

> La Donna mobile
> My legs are wobb-ely . . .
> No bloomin' wo-ender
> Look what they're u-ender!

There were sniggers too about the luckless Mrs. McGuire, who
apparently didn't know where to put herself, as the saying goes.

> Mrs. McGuire sat on the fire
> The fire was too hot, she sat on a pot
> The pot was too wide, so she sat on the Clyde
> And a' the wee fishes ran up her backside.
> Th'were all sorts of wee rude things you could say too . . . Not bad
> things really, but your mother didn't like to hear you say 'Christopher
> Columbus!' . . . near swearing she thought that was.

She might have been a deal more horrified if she had heard her
offspring giving lip to the guardian of the law himself. It was no
doubt lucky for them that he kept his cliping for more serious or
dangerous offences.

> When I lived in Cumberland Street, it was teeming wi' lads. We played
> ever'thing right enough but specially footb'll. Then we'd get chased by
> big Rab the policeman . . . and we'd make faces and yell things at him.
>   'Yous are awful cheeky gettin'. I'll tell your Ma's'
> But he might just give you a skelp on the bahoochie and tell you no'to
> play footb'll in the street. He never did tell your Ma . . . just gave you
> lalldy again the next time. Then till he was round the corner you just
> played keepie-uppie in a close.

If Rab the Cumberland Street policeman didn't clipe, other
malicious peers did. But not without retribution. Jack Roche
wished a vicious fate on his enemy, that had been common
currency to almost all rememberers.

> Tell-tale tit, your tongue shall be slit
> And all the doggies in the town will get a little bit.

And there was slander on the clipe's family too.

Tell-tale tit, your Mammy cannae knit
Your Da, he cannae go to bed
Wi'oot a dummy-tit.

More deadly still in any controversy (though it took Peggy Carson a while to know what it meant) was the put-down . . .

Your Mammy couldnae run a menauge!*

Actually, since Mammy was no doubt running a family of seven or eight, managing a capricious range and stretching a thin wage to gossamer, running a menauge would have been child's play. Peggy had another wee puzzle when she was only a Mixed Infant and telling a tall story. Then her granny was in for it too.

'Och, your Granny's mutch!' someone'd say.
But-here my granny *did* wear a mutch and I didnae know what that had to do wi' me telling a wee fib.

Squabbling, name-calling, sworn best-friendships, feuds and mild vendettas kaleidoscoped and slotted in and out of the bosom-partnerships of childhood . . . but always within a loose grouping in their own stamping grounds, but as they left peever and cigarettes cards behind, they began to sample the activities that would engross some of them in adult life, and to stretch their wings into other districts.

When we were in the big school we used to go swimming . . . in your one-piece costume down to your knees . . . went to the baths down the Green. You took your chittering bites for after, too. A biscuit or maybe a slice of soft toast from breakfast time. I still like a bit of soft toast so I do.

Mr. Jimmy Dewar went to the Pollokshaws baths.

You used to go past the steamie women doing their washing, along the corridor with the smell of chlorine wafting towards you and the moving green reflections on the water as you got near the pond . . .

* A 'menauge' was an arrangement in which a group pooled a sum from each week's pay, one among them in turn getting the total pooled.

Sometimes if you were swimming in a school gala you got taken through the steamie and down the stair to a kind of basement to get a mug of Bovril.

And a chuckling eavesdropper adds a memory that has stayed with him for over sixty years.

I mind wandering by mistake into the Turkish bath place, and–here th'was a lot of fat, bare women with towels round their heads sittin' in clouds of steam. That was a sight I tell you!

And what about this for sheer whole-heartedness in learning to swim?

I was well up before I learned and this fella in the pub, he says to me he says, 'You cannae swim! Away t'the chemist and buy a pair o' water-wings' So I gets my Captain Webb's Wings and goes to the Greenhead baths. I learned quite quick and later I was in the Scottish championships . . . breast stroke. I still swim . . . 9 o'clock every Sunday morning.

But at ninety Alex Donnelly does confess to being taken by car.

Swimming was all-the-year-round of course, but when the summer came it might be 'anyone for tennis?'

There was an old empty house, a ha'pennyworth on the green tram from us, and it had a kind of rough tennis-court. We used to take wir bats and play there. The lines was all gone so th'was a right lot of squabbling. It was good but, that tennis.

Golf too had its learner devotees . . . on a better site certainly than the run-down tennis-court, but hampered a little in the matter of equipment.

We'd a set of golf sticks in our house and I'd two brothers and two friends. When it was quiet the greenie at the Corporation golf course used to let us in on the one ticket because there was just the one set of sticks in the old bag. That was dandy.

Miss Isobel Horn's early days as a golfer started more conventionally at a bona fide club.

What was Radleigh School later on, was once the Williamwood Ladies' Golf Clubhouse and my friend Keith Ramage and I got joining as junior members. We couldn't have been more than eight. We must have been like two wee rabbits scuttling about the course.

When ponds were 'bearing', skating with blades that they clamped on to their shoes was a favourite ploy. So was cycling . . . in earnest, on organised excursions . . . and rambling. They all had their enthusiasts.

> I was in a cycling club . . . be about 1912. I can remember going out in my white stockings, a wide frilly cotton dress and even a hat . . . a flowery straw hat that you let down your back when you were on the bike. It was that silly really, the white . . . because you always came home with oil on your stockings or on your dress.

Even for those who couldn't rise to a fifth of a set of golf sticks or a tennis bat and certainly not a bike, there was always the likes of the plain running that set Bobby Ford up for a long-term interest.

> There wasn't much 'playing' for me when I was wee. There was too much work on the croft. But I did exercises to make me grow . . . I was very small. And I did a lot of running. Twice I won the quarter mile at the county sports, and then in Glasgow I was always in a club. The Coplawhill Running Club met at the park in Elmvale Street. Best wee park in Glasgow.

But above and beyond them all there was what, to a man, they all called 'footb'll'. They followed their teams, of course, and chanted their rhymes . . .

> Jock McGraw, he never saw
> Where Alan Morton pit the ba' . . .

and others less polite. They played their own games in back-courts, school yards, parks . . . and on the street with bundled jackets for goal-posts. The street could be a hazardous pitch, not so much for the threat of carts or carriages, but because of vigilant and over zealous policemen. Mrs. Mysie Kyle is still indignant on her husband's behalf, indignant enough to keep a treasured document safe in a plastic folder.

> I kept it from 1923. It's from the City Police Department charging him and two other boys with playing football in Wishart Street . . . 'to the obstruction and annoyance of the lieges' whoever they may be! The penalty was to be a twenty shilling fine or *ten days in jail*. That would've been Barlinnie. Just for kicking a wee rubber ball about! The policeman used to have his cup of tea at the Necropolis gate-house and he came out and chased them down the road into the arms of another policeman.

A slip-up over the date of the alleged felony happily saved the boys from either the then huge fine of twenty shillings or the ten days in Barlinnie. But after seventy years his wife is still in shock.

Twenty shillings . . . ten days in jail!

So we'll leave 'playing', with the ninety-four-year-old yearning for her chuckies and another, not much younger, wishing she had the coalie-plant recipe. The years were passing for those youngsters of the early century and beyond, and as the finish of little Christina Rodgers' palmy days brought a previous chapter to an end, we'll let one of Jack Roche's memories draw this one to a close. He was done now with pulling his sleeve over his fist if the teacher made him join hands with a girl in a circle-game . . . he was almost ready to look at them in a new light.

In the school we'd a wee rhyme we tormented the girls with . . .
Doh Ray Mi, when I was wee
I used to pare the tatties-o
Now I am big, and I can dig
And I can kiss the lassies-o.

And that was them, readier than they knew, for the next of the Seven Ages of Man, and the ongoings they would store up as memories of their courting days.

19

I was a Shabbos Goy

It was all very much you didn't do this and you didn't do that on Sundays. Oh no! You did nothing on the Sabbath. It was the day of rest.

Or was it? For all that resting and refraining, it seems that what they did do occupied every hour and minute of the day.

You didn't play or read ordinary books or anything on Sunday. It was taken up with church and Sunday School and Boy's Brigade, and walking to the services at Langside Hill. That was from the Round Toll at Pollokshaws to the church at the Battlefield monument. That church's just a shell now, but I've an old photo of it and the place beside it where the house stood that they called Queen Mary's cottage. That's where she got resting at the time of the Battle of Langside.

If you did those two miles back and forward two or three times a Sunday, there wouldn't be much leisure left to chafe at the long hours hanging on your hands. In the opposite direction to the one the Dewars took, trooped the Hutchison clan. Ann Hutchison remembers . . .

On Sundays we walked from Pleasance Street away up to Eastwood Church. That was quite far when you were wee. You'd always your best clo'es on . . . your good dress or coat. After the church th'was the Sunday School in the hall beside the cemetery.

Whether or not that was regarded or feared as an intimation of mortality she doesn't add, but goes on . . .

That was what we called the Morning Meeting. I got a prize there . . . a Bible. We'd wee texts to learn from cards, but I don't think I ever got a prize for that. It would've been the good attendance wi' me, not the texts.

One of the kenspeckle worthies around Pollokshaws that she might have passed on her way to Eastwood Church was the 'rival' Secession minister recalled by her neighbour.

> He was a figure that fascinated me because of his clothes. He wore a big Father Brown hat with a brim and a sort of frock coat like Chairman Mao.

For many others, like Mysie Kyle, morning kirk was far from being the only diet of worship.

> We'd two lots of Sunday School as well, one at eleven before the church and another at five o'clock . . . and the evening service. We went to them all. There was nothing else to do.

Janet Kay recalls precisely where she sat in their church, over seventy years ago.

> I went to the two o'clock service with my mother and father . . . sat between them. He was a deacon. We sat in Gallery-pew number 116 I remember.

The journey to church wasn't always as sedate as the procession of Dewars and Hutchisons at Pollokshaws . . . not even for adults. Jimmy Dewar's granny (who must have been born in the middle of last century) had a special dispensation for her Sunday cantrips. She lived with a son a mile or two and several hills away from her kirk, and there was nothing in the Shorter Catechism to answer a little personal moral problem she had.

> My uncle used to take her in his motor-bike sidecar. She was worried about the propriety of that and asked the minister if it was quite decent. Dr. Chisholm just laughed and told her 'of course' and then she was quite happy.

But the Catechism did answer many religious queries. And however imperfectly it was understood by the young of the flock, like the Struan Yule of tender years, in later days the 'jargon' had shaken itself down into comprehensible and wise counsel.

> I remember doing the Catechism. It was difficult then, but I've always been grateful for it as a man.

John Adamson looks back too and considers the delayed-action value of the rote question-and-answer that seemed so pointless at the time.

> Oh aye. In my day it was the Catechism and all that. 'What's Man's chief end? and so on. Then you answered, 'To glorify God and enjoy Him for ever'. Didn't know what it meant then, but funny . . . it's like the Psalms you learned, you find them quite a lot coming into your mind when you're grown-up . . . and all of a sudden you know fine what they mean.

So there was, in those remembered years, a general mood of strictness and convention. Yet here and there were some who were not quite so thirled to jot and tittle of the Law and the Prophets. The Lockie family were allowed one or two not particularly religious pursuits on the Sabbath. Maybe *ever* so slightly Bohemian were the Lockies . . . but only after the correct observances had been made.

> I went to Sunday School of course, in my Sunday best . . . always dressed. I find it difficult at eighty-nine to change from the wee gracious nice ways that used to be normal. Anyway, after the Church and Sunday School we did other things. Our family being musical and 'arty' we had music . . . not just hymns . . . and did a bit of sketching and watercolour painting. We were a bit kind of liberal, I suppose.

Even in earlier twentieth century days than the eighties and nineties, there was a small Muslim population in Glasgow for whom Friday, not Sunday, was Prayers day. Indeed there's an old jingle to remind of the various holy days observed by different religious groups in the city.

> Christians worship God on Sunday,
> Grecian zealots hallow Monday,
> Assyrians Wednesday revere,
> Egyptians, Thursday . . . Friday, Turks.
> On Saturday no Hebrew works.

That last was true of the Balarsky family certainly, and Mrs. Lily Balarsky has warm memories of the Jewish Shabbos.

In winter on Friday we used to get out of school a wee bit early to get home in time to do all the traditional things. We were sent to Callender's big bakehouse in Hospital Street, where the night before we would've put in the Shabbos dinner for cooking in the enormous oven there. That dinner was the 'cholent'. It was a traditional kind of hot-pot. Abie Callender had come from Poland as a boy and he'd worked his way up to having this bakehouse. The whole family worked in it and delivered bread, schaltz herring and wurst in an ancient van to Jewish families all over Glasgow. There was a non-Jewish driver of course (had to be to work on the Shabbos) but he'd picked up quite a bit of Yiddish during his deliveries because a lot of Jewish people then had very little English.

Carrying the cholent home was forbidden manual labour so that job was done by a willing non-Jewish neighbour, with the little Lily running alongside sniffing like a Bisto kid. Another friend pressed into service between Friday and Saturday dusk would be a 'Shabbos goy' who would see to the cleaning out and lighting of the Jewish household fire. Jimmy Dewar was a 'goy boy' in his young days.

> When I was a message-boy at week-ends I often went in to do the fire in Jewish households. Sometimes I got a penny or tuppence . . . maybe ev'n more. The Shapiros were a nice family like that.

That 'cholent' would be a sociable meal eaten round the Shabbos goy's fire. But it wasn't always hot-pot that was on the menu. Sometimes it was a tender treat supplied by someone called the Hen Lady.

> It was the Bensons in the Gorbals who supplied poultry specially for Jewish households. Mrs. Benson was a widow and we called her the Hen Lady. Her son and daughter bought hens from the farms round Glasgow and took them to the Jewish slaughter-house . . . the shacht, off Norfolk Street. Then she would come round her customers. In our close it was my mother's house she came to, and we used to pull the other bells to tell everyone that the Hen Lady was there. She weighed them out using your mother's bags of sugar and packets of tea as weights.

She went away after this communal marketing and left the women to their tea and strudel and a good blether.

When the hen-killing Bensons graduated to having a shop in Crown Street, a move vividly recalled by Mrs. Balarsky, the bell-ringing became only a memory, but the cosy chat flitted to the Gorbals.

> I used to get sent to the shop. There was live poultry in cages all round and you queued for your hen and listened to the Yiddish gossip. They used to singe the feathers off at a gas jet that was lit all the time . . . and I remember getting told to mind that I had the giblets safe in my newspaper parcel of hen.

So much for Jewish cultural rituals. But there were Christian customs too, though then as now, not all branches of the church had the same emphases, but Sabbath-day food is remembered by all denominations as 'special' after the mince and turnips and tapioca of the workaday week. Mario Servadei recalls the Italian Catholic Sunday with the social obligations and good eating that were slotted in and around church attendance . . . and shatters a little illusion.

> There was church, always church. Then after that the Italians visited relatives . . . had a special meal . . . maybe chicken, which was quite a treat in those days. Not so much pasta. Italians don't eat as much pasta as people think.

And Peggy Carson . . .

> We'd maybe just sausages or stew through the week but there was always a wee bit roast beef for your Sunday dinner, and then we went to my granny's for tea and always had an iced cake wi' a base of jam and pastry . . . an Albert cake. I cannae think on my granny wi'out seeing that Albert cake.

On the lively Christian wing were the Missioners whose meetings were a bright haven for the hard-worked farm family from Govan.

> We didn't have special clothes for Sunday. There was never enough for that for all of us. So we didn't always get to the church. But we did go to the Paddy Black Mission. We sang choruses there. Y'know the sort of thing, 'I will make you fishers of men' and 'He did not come to judge the world'. And there was 'I'm H.A.P.P.Y.' I always mind those and I still hum them to myself after seventy-five years.

They were H.A.P.P.Y. at a mission in Springburn too.

> Th'was a tram conductor and his wife ran a mission here. 'Seth and Beth' we used to call them. I don't think that was really their names, but the second name was Sykes right-enough. I liked the mission and bawling out the choruses to the piano.

On the other hand, there were grave worshippers with no piano, but who sat under a precentor with his choir and tuning-fork. They were sticklers for what was 'fitting' and would have thought it blasphemy to use the actual words of the Psalmist in their midweek practices. To skirt this problem they resorted to metrical psalm 'ditties' not to confuse worship with rehearsal, which was no doubt as po-faced a performance as that on the Sabbath.

> O mother dear, John Laurie's lum
> When shall it sweepit be?
> For a' the soot right doon it's come
> And spoilt my Granny's tea.

There's a niggling thought that David himself might just have taken a wee staw at such parody. There were other inhibitions too at choir practices.

> The beadle that was the grave-digger as well, sang in the choir with my uncle and he used to say, 'you cannae ask folk how they're keepin' for fear they think you're lookin' to a fee for turnin' ower their grave sods'.

There's a persistent notion of more modern times that for the whole sixty-odd years of the Victorian age, man lost his sense of humour and the absurd, under the impact of a few Sabbatarians. But healthy people are seldom so brainwashed that wit and laughter die on the tongue. In those sober days they were simply enjoyed around moral matters, or rose from the observances themselves. There's many a quiet chuckle among those who remember how much fun came from church life itself.

> I remember in the Sunday School the class being told the story of Mary and Joseph going on the journey into Egypt from Bethlehem. Then they'd to draw a picture of the story. One wee girl had the three of them, Mary on the donkey, Joseph leading it, and a little chap walking alongside carrying a suitcase with the initials J.C. on it.

And Mr. Alistair Cook recalls a generous mite he once put into the Sunday School collecting bag.

> I put in an I.O.U. for a million pounds. I put in a button too and the next week the Superintendent stood up with a dead serious face. 'Thanks very much,' he says, 'to the generous boy or girl who put in such a handsome offering last Sunday'.

He laughs at the recollection and adds . . .

> I'm still trying to pay off that debt in the same church.

A more seriously intended I.O.U. heard about by Jack Roche, was once put on to the plate by a farmer on Glasgow's rural fringe.

> This old boy put in an I.O.U. for a whole pig. My grandpa came from the country and he said it wasnae all that unusual for farmers to promise a bit of money after the next market day. But a pig! He said as well that it was a recognised thing in his old kirk that if the collection was small they just gave it to the beadle . . . a perk like.

A head appears from behind the wing of an armchair in the retirement-complex lounge.

> My father used to tell a story about a minister he knew, scolding his congregation for just putting five-and-tenpence in the plate the week before. 'Heaven's a long ways away,' says-he. 'You'll no' get there for five-and-tenpence'.

It's hard to visualise a Sunday School nativity play ending in chaos.

> I mind hearing about a wee chap that was the Innkeeper. Right wee caution he must've been. Maybe he just forgot his bit or maybe it was just devilment, but when Joseph asked if th'was' any room at the inn' he threw a spanner in the rest of the play when he says, 'Oh aye, plenty room!'

Although most people found humour, warmth and friendship in their kirks and congregations, and in the organisations that kept them together during the week, there were places where pleasure was hard to find.

> After a nice minister that encouraged social things we got one that wouldn't let you do anything . . . not even a Sale of Work, never mind a social . . . no making money and friends at the same time for him! And he put down the football team. He was a right hell-and-thunder man.

Mysie Kyle voted on him with her feet and took her custom to Montrose Street Congregational Church where her young man was a leader in the Boys' Brigade. The B.B. still inspires the loyalty of the very elderly who joined it when it was still a young organisation, and many a man sitting in an Eventide home sports the anchor badge in his lapel even now.

> My father was connected with the Woodside Mission when William Smith started the Boys' Brigade. It was a rare thing for boys. I think it was the B.B. that gave me a bit of discipline.

. . . or perhaps the mother that saw to the white trimmings and sent him off to its meetings. Not long after him, another rememberer was sprucing himself up for B.B. night.

> I was in the B.B. in its quite early days. It was started about 1883 and I would be in it twenty years after that, wi' my wee pill-box, my belt and haversack and a dummy rifle for drill. Later it was my suit and a Glengarry . . . just your Sunday suit, no' a uniform. But you'd to have a straight shed in your hair and it all sleeked back.

Their sisters weren't far behind them.

> I was in the Girls' Guildry, the Glasgow 29th. We wore a white blouse and a blue skirt, and a red sash with pom-poms at the end. We'd round felt hats too.

Peggy Carson was a Brigade lass too.

> We did crafts and things, and bar-bell exercises like yon . . . what d'you cry them . . . majorettes is it?

Many a mother who ran a tight family ship and sent her young out to the uniformed organisations hailed the Band of Hope too, as a power for good, *and* took the pledge herself.

> I was a Little White Ribboner of the British Women's Temperance Association. The 'ribbon' was a wee brooch in the form of a bow. There was a lot of public drunkenness when I was young and some women lived a life of hell with men that drank their wages and came in at the end of the week with nothing. Some of the women went to the Works gate to wait for their men.

Mrs. Agnes Grove's family favoured another temperance organisation, The Order of Rechabites.

> I went to that as a juvenile. You paid three ha'pence a week, a penny for funeral benefit and a ha'penny for the doctor . . . a kind of wee insurance. If you brought in four members you got a badge with 'Faith, Hope, Truth and Love' on it and round the edge 'We drink no wine'.

Wine or not, they could kick up their heels with the best and while mothers were knitting tea-cosies for bazaars, and fathers organising the juveniles as Sons of Rechab . . .

. . . we'd rare dances once a month at the Rechabites' Good Templars' Lodge.

As well as the week-night meetings connected with church life there were Saturday activities for the likes of Jimmy Dewar, provided by well-meaning philanthropists.

There was a Peacock's bakery and rooms in Shawlands and we used to have tea and buns there after a sort of mission youth meeting in the Waverley cinema . . . paid for by the Jam man at Carluke who was far-ben with the evangelicals.

On summer Saturdays there were Sunday School picnics. In a more sophisticated age when the young are as familiar as their elders with half-a-dozen different international cuisines, it's difficult to imagine the thrill of counting off the days until *the trip* . . . of seeing your pinafore starched, of putting a new string on your tinnie and blanco-ing your san'shoes till they were powdery and stiff.

We used to get the tram, a special tram for the trip. and go to Spiersbridge. There was the burn and a field behind the tea-room. And there was a big corrugated barn we went into if it rained.

From the Paddy Black Mission the young Rodgers went to their trip on a coal lorry.

The horses got all decorated and the lorries scrubbed. You just stood up there, holding on to each other and the horses gallopin' away . . . your tins dangling . . . away ready for your races . . . See when you think on it . . . running races for prizes, knockin' your breath out for a wee bun!

Not all Sunday School trips were smiled on by kirky parents. Jimmy Dewar had just a single experience of one of those.

There was a Socialist Sunday School in Pollokshaws, connected someway with the Co-op. My friend Charlie Brown (that lived in one of the single-ends with wooden stairs and landing, and an old well outside at the back), anyway Charlie went to the Socialist Sunday School. My mother didn't like that connection at all. I went with him to a picnic at Saltcoats . . . oh you carried on at a church trip, but that one was a lot wilder. Charlie Brown was clever . . . became a doctor.

Perhaps it's because the old kirks don't mean so much to even the earnest young of the 1990s, the ones who still 'do justice, love mercy and walk humbly' but *without* their God, that old antagonisms are fading between the two largest denominations. Of course there are still the diehards, those who hold fiercely to their own certainties; but few youngsters confront each other now with the old provocative question 'A Billy or a Dan or an old tin can?' to pick a fight with the opposition. Perhaps because there are more agnostic 'old tin cans'.

> I'm a Roman Catholic but I used to like to see the Orange Walk when I was young . . . the drums and whistles y'know? I remember once making my father's hair stand on end by coming in saying how I'd watched it and *waved*.

Eileen Reilly too, found denominational edges blurred on a small embarrassing adventure she once had.

> I went with a friend to a Catholic teachers' meeting in the City Chambers. We went up the marble staircase and 'mingled', eating the nice wee sandwiches and sipping the sherry . . . ever so genteel. Then I caught sight of this man in lace frills and cuffs and black breeches, and I knew it was the Moderator of the Church of Scotland Assembly! and that we must be at a Protestant church reception. We slunk back down the staircase past the flunkies and hot-footed it to the City *Hall* for the right meeting . . . no sherry and nibbles there though.

Perhaps we should close the door on religious affiliations with that ecumenical jaunt, and end with the last few lines from a poem by Struan Yule who, in spite of pinging ink wads at the Whitehill Paddies of his youth, grew up quite literate and took to composing verse. In writing of deep denominational division in time past, he finishes . . .

> But now today's Geneva gown
> At ease with priestly stole, kneels down
> To thank the Lord who made this town
> The Dear Green Place
> That flourishes, to wear the crown
> Of civic grace.

Glossary

Airts	Directions	*Cadge*	Beg: Carry
All-his-orders	Bits and pieces	*Canoodle*	Cuddle
An'all	Too	*Cantrips*	Ongoings
Argy-bargy	Argue	*Caur*	Car, tram
Arle	Contract by coin	*Causeys*	Cobbles
A.R.P.	Air raid Precautions	*Caution*	Winning child
A.T.S.	Auxiliary Territorial Service	*Caw*	Turn
		Champ	Strain; Mash
Aye	Yes; Always	*Chanter*	Finger part of bagpipes
Ayont	Beyond	*Chap*	Knock
		Chenille	Cloth with velvety nap (Fr. Caterpillar)
Bahoochie	Backside		
Baikie	Ash-can	*Cheuch-jean*	Twist of toffee
Ba' on the slates	Game over	*Chink*	Gap
		Chitter	Shiver
Bawbee	Halfpenny	*Chuckie*	Small stone
B.E.F.	British Expeditionary Force	*Clachan*	Village
		Clawt	Fire rake
Belt	Punishment by strap	*Cleek*	Hook
Biddy	Lady teacher	*Cleekit*	Hooked
Bien	Well-off	*Cley dod*	Clay marble
Bierers	Bedstead slats	*Clinker*	Stoney cinder
Billy	Protestant	*Clipe*	Tell-tale
Blether	Chatter	*Cludgie*	W.C.
Bogie	Plank on wheels	*Cock-a-snook*	Defy
Bool	Marble	*Cocky*	Saucy, pert
Brae	Hill	*Coont*	Count
Braws	Best clothes	*Coort*	Court
Breeks	Trousers	*Coup*	Spill
Bumphlie	Rumpled, bulky	*Couthy*	Comfortable
Bundy	Time-clock	*Craik*	Whine for
Bunnet	Cap	*Cran*	Crane
Burn	Stream	*Cry*	Call, name
Byne	Basin	*Cubby*	Small cupboard
		Cuddy	Horse

Dan	R. Catholic	*Gizinties*	Arithmetic
Darg	Laborious task	*Glaur*	Mud
Dawd	Lump, clod	*Glebe*	Manse land
Dawdle	Linger	*Glob*	Globule
Dook	Immerse	*Gir', Gird*	Hoop
Doo	Pigeon	*Going-your-*	Going-at-it
Doo-lander	Flat cap	*dinger*	hard
Douce	Prim	*Goy*	Non-Jew
Dreep	Drop by finger-tips	*Grieve*	Farm foreman
		Grue	Shudder
Driv	Drove		
Dry	Unlicensed for sale of alcohol	*Haddie*	Haddock
		Hap	Wrap
Duds	Clothes	*Haud*	Hold
Dunkey-man	Ship's greaser	*Heed*	Pay attention
Dunt	Knock, blow	*Heedrum-*	Bagpipe music
Dunny	Low area	*hodrums*	
Dyke	Wall	*Heid-bummer*	Boss
		Hen	Pet name for female
Easy-osie	Lackadaisical	*Het*	'It' in a game
		Hing	Hang (at window)
Fankle	Mix-up	*Humph*	Carry bulky object
Far-ben	Deeply involved	*Hurdy-gurdy*	Barrel-organ
Feart	Afraid	*Hurl*	Wheel
Fender	Kerb	*Hurlie*	Bed on wheels
Flet	Pour tea into saucer		
		Jannie	Janitor
Flit	Move house	*Jaurie*	Stone marble
Flummox	Bewilder	*Jaw-box*	Sink
Fly	Shrewd	*Jiggin'*	Dancing
Flype	Turn inside-out	*Jing-bang*	Whole thing
Flyte	Scold		
Foozled	Bamboozled	*Keepie-uppie*	Keeping ball in the air
Forby (e)	As well		
		Ken	Know
Galumphing	Romping, barging	*Kenspeckle*	Well-known by sight
Gaunie	Will you please.	*Kee-hoy*	Hide-and-seek
Geggie	Magic lantern	*Kidding*	Teasing
Genteel	Refined	*Kilter*	Order
Gey	Very	*Kybosh*	Put a halt to
Ghoulie	Ghostly		
Gie	Give	*Laching*	Laughing
Ginger	Any kind of lemonade	*Lalldy*	Punishment
		Loof	Hand

Lum	Chimney		lozenges
Lumber	Boy/girl friend	*Relict*	Widow
		Roastin'	Fierce telling-of:
McCallum	Ice-cream with raspberry sauce	*Runty*	Worthless
Majolica	Green/blue/fawn pottery	*Sapple*	Soapsuds
Malarky	Mischief	*Scart*	Scratch
Mealie-puddin'	Oatmeal and suet in skin	*Scoosh*	Chute of water
		Scuddy	Naked
Midden	Rubbish tip	*Scullery*	Kitchen
Midgie	Dustbin	*Semmit*	Vest
Mind	Remember	*Shabbos*	Sabbath
Mooch	Scrounge: Loiter	*Shacht*	Slaughter-house
Moshie	Game with marbles	*Shed*	Hair-parting
		Shoogly	Shaky
Naething	Nothing	*Shorgun*	Short gown
Nane	None	*Shot*	Turn
Nyaff	Insignificant person	*Sine, syne*	Rinse
		Single-end	One-room-house
O.C.T.U.	Officer-Cadet Training Unit	*Skiddle*	Play about with water
Oose	Fluff	*Skint*	Hard-up
Out-of-kilter	Disordered	*Skite*	Slip, slide
Oxter	Armpit	*Sklim*	Climb
		Slider	Ice-cream wafer
Paddy	Male teacher	*Slitter*	Messy work (-er)
Palmy	A blow on the hand	*Smeddum*	Vigour
		Sod	Turf, clod
Pan-loaf	Posh	*Sook*	Suck
Pare	Peel	*Soor*	Sour
Peerie	Spinning-top	*Soor-dook*	Buttermilk
Peever	Hopscotch	*Spirtle*	Stirring-rod
Piece	Rough sandwich	*Staw*	Grudge, aversion
Pinnie, peenie	Pinafore	*Steamie*	Public wash-house
Pinsil	Pencil	*Steep*	Soak
Poentry	Poetry (pure Glasgow)	*Stint*	Period of work
		Stookie	Stiff
Poind, pon', pawn)	Lace point, bed trim	*Stot*	Bounce
		Stotious	Very drunk
Poke	Paper-bag	*Stroup*	Spout
Pokey-hat	Ice-cream cone	*Sugarollie*	Liquorice
Press	Shallow cupboard	*Swank*	Show-off
		Swop	Exchange
Rammy	Row		
Readin' sweeties	Conversation	*Tate*	Small quantity

Tattie, tottie	Potato
Taury	Tarry
Teabread	Scones and buns
Tenter	Loom attendant
Teuchter	Highlander
Thibbet	Coarse cloth
Thirled	Tied
Thole	Endure
Thon, thonder	Yon, yonder
Thrapple	Throat
Tim	Empty
Trams	Horse shafts
Trim'ly	Trembling
Turn-your-wilkies	Somersault
Under-duds	Underwear
Unfankled	Unravelled
Wally close	Ceramic tiled close
Weel-aff	Rich; All right
What-for	Scolding, punishment
Wheeching	Rushing
Winching	Courting (wenching)
Windie	Window

A DAY IN THE DEATH OF JOE EGG

After National Service in India, Malaya and Hong Kong, Peter Nichols acted in repertory and TV before becoming a teacher. He has written some twenty original plays and adaptations for TV, six feature films and the following stage plays: *A Day in the Death of Joe Egg, The National Health, Forget-me-not Lane, The Freeway, Chez Nous, Privates on Parade, Born in the Gardens, Passion Play, Poppy, Blue Murder* and *A Piece of My Mind*. He has won five Evening Standard Awards, two Best Musical Awards and a Society of West End Theatre Award for Best Comedy. He was resident playwright at the Guthrie Theatre, Minneapolis, where he co-directed *The National Health*. He also directed revivals of *Joe Egg* and *Forget-me-not Lane* at Greenwich. In 1967 he shared the John Whiting Award with Peter Terson. His book of memoirs, *Feeling You're Behind*, was published in 1984.